FROM OLD STREETS TO NEW HOMES

A Memoir of Derry, Bridge Street and Shantallow

Tony Hassan

©2023 Tony Hassan
Layout/design by Neil Roddy - www.fudgedesigns.co.uk
Printed by Bizzprint

The moral rights of the authors and contributors have been asserted in accordance with
the Copyright, Designs and Patents Act, 1998.
First published November 2023.
Colmcille Press, Ráth Mór Centre, Derry BT48 0LZ
Managing Editor Garbhán Downey
www.colmcillepress.com

Colmcille Press gratefully acknowledges the support of Creggan Enterprises Limited
and the John Bryson Foundation.

RÁTH MÓR
Creggan Enterprises

The John Bryson
Foundation

ISBN 978-1-914009-39-6
A CIP copy for this book is available from the British Library.

This book is dedicated to my family and my many friends and comrades over the years, all of whom made me the person I am today.

In particular, to my sister Ann - who was everything to us - and who died on 4 December 2017 and will never be forgotten.

Suaimhneas síoraí ar a hanam dílis.

All proceeds from this book will be donated to the Foyle Hospice.

Tony Hassan

Acknowledgements

There is a team of people who deserve my deepest gratitude for helping me during the writing of this book. First and foremost, my wife Christine has been a rock of support at every stage, as have my children Ciarán and Áine, and my nieces Caoimhe and Mairéad Fox.

Julieann Campbell was a source of great advice and guidance, as were my publishers Joe Martin and Garbhán Downey of Colmcille Press, and Chris McDonagh and Minty Thompson of Greater Shantallow Area Partnership (GSAP). Many thanks also to Mitchel McLaughlin, who showed great generosity to my work by penning such a kind and comprehensive Foreword. My sincere appreciation also to those who contributed financial and practical support, and helped make this book a reality:

Derry City & Strabane District Council Arts & Culture Department
Martin Sheehan
Rory McPartland and Darren Kirby of GSAP
Joe McGinnis and Vincent Bradley of Braidwater
Liam Clifford of Racecourse Stores
Paddy MacDermott Solicitor
Dominic O'Kane
Sean McGlinchey
George Long
Councillor John McGowan and
Peter McDonald.

Míle buíochas daoibh go léir.

About the Author

Derry man Tony Hassan spent decades as a Sinn Féin activist, and, later, as an elected representative trying to create meaningful change in the city he loves so well. Now retired, Tony was a community activist during some of the darkest days of the conflict and was instrumental in many of the major housing developments to transform Derry since the peace process.

A father of two and grandfather of seven, Tony retired from politics in 2018 and lives with his wife, Chrissie, and family in Derry in the north of Ireland.

Contents

FOREWORD
By Mitchel McLaughlin

My overwhelming impression when reading a draft copy of Tony Hassan's Memoir was admiration for the dedication of the author and astonishment at his powers of recall of events that shaped his life and indeed the broader contemporary history of Derry.

The opening chapters outline a city in the post-war era, whose economic potential had been strangled by the denial of civil rights and the gerrymandering of the electoral process. which enabled a minority of voters to dominate local Government and obstruct educational and economic opportunity for non-Unionists. This pernicious policy extended to a systemic abuse of housing provision also.

Notwithstanding this experience, the author has written a vivid account of living in a happy and stable household in the Bridge Street and Orchard Street district of Derry, despite inevitable decay and dereliction, created and sustained by deliberate institutional neglect.

This narrative will remind readers of the strength of community and familial relationships and the ability to overcome many obstacles to progressive reform and, in addition, provides an engaging commentary of educational provision, especially as provided under the dominating influence of the Church.

Today the sixties are internationally characterised as an era of social liberation, including throughout the island of Ireland. Again, the writer demonstrates a very sharp recall of early adulthood, the experience of employment as well as unemployment and the vicissitudes of repeated redundancy and an ongoing pursuit of paid employment whilst living in an economic blackspot.

Clearly as a young adult, the author experienced the early 1960s as a great time to be alive and was as oblivious as everyone else, to the conflict that was about to convulse society in the north of Ireland, including and perhaps especially his hometown of Derry.

In due course, the inevitable happened when on October 5th, 1968, a Civil Rights march, previously banned by the Unionist regime, was viciously attacked by the RUC.

Life for everyone living on the Island of Ireland and especially in the North, was changed irrevocably that day.

Again and again, the author maps the course of subsequent events with unusual clarity of memory and understanding.

1969 – The Battle of the Bogside and the deployment of the British Army. Entire streets burned out by loyalists as Belfast republicans rioted in solidarity with Derry.

1971 – Getting married to Christine in Dublin and the eventual process of settling in Derry and bringing up a young family in what had effectively become a war zone.

1972 – Internment, Bloody Sunday, followed by Operation Motorman and the author's life-changing decision to join Sinn Féin. The prison struggle of the 70s and 80s and consequent welfare support and transport facilities for families meant unremitting and ongoing fund-raising and the author explains how concerts and bingo sessions were organised to sustain the work of the Prisoners' Dependants' Fund in the Derry area. He also describes the establishment of an Incident Centre, a refurbished caravan, which was parked opposite the Shops in Shantallow and operated for several years before a permanent office was obtained.

1980 & 1981 – Hunger Strikes, and the global media begin, at last, to investigate the conflict in Ireland and the terrible consequences of repression of national and civil rights. The elections of Bobby Sands, Paddy Agnew and Kieran Doherty were a shattering blow to the Thatcher policy of criminalisation of the prisoners. Subsequent electoral advances, especially in the Local Government Elections (1985) forced Maggie Thatcher's Government to introduce ever more desperate measures.

The British government's broadcasting ban, which basically censored the voices of elected republican and loyalist activists on TV and radio lasted from 1988 until 1994 before collapsing in ignominy as the Sinn Féin electoral success continued.

This review of recent history also reflects the emerging Peace Process as buoyed by a strengthening electoral mandate, Sinn Féin published its

Peace proposals (Scenario for Peace & Towards A Lasting Peace In Ireland). The author skilfully explains the outworking of the Peace Process and subsequent initiatives by republicans to maximise the new opportunities for an honourable peace in our country.

This book provides an invaluable insight into almost 50 years of political struggle for Irish self-determination. There are many activists with an established public profile and many, many more who deserve to be recognised.

Tony Hassan's book is an acknowledgement of them all.

Mitchel McLaughlin is the retired National Chairperson of Sinn Féin and former Speaker/Ceann Comhairle of the Stormont Assembly.

CHAPTER 1
FAMILY TIES

I feel I have lived through the best and the worst of Derry. It's my hometown and a place I appreciate now more than ever as I look back at our lives here.

Bridge Street, which ran up the hill from the river, was a fantastic old street and a real adventure for us growing up in the 1950s. I was brought up and reared at Number 55 - the eldest son of Gerard and Margaret Hassan. My father, Gerry, was a docker. My mother, Maggie, was a housewife, dressmaker, and the best cook in Ireland! My brother Desmond was a year younger, and when my sister Ann came along in 1951, our family of five was complete.

My father's family originally hailed from the countryside in the Feeny/Terrydreen area of County Derry, a place we visited many times as youngsters. My mother, however, was a Scotch woman from Glasgow who had met my father in Buncrana at what was called the Scotch Fair - when people from Glasgow came over to County Donegal for their holidays. This usually lasted for two weeks, and thus began their romance. My mother's maiden name was McGuire, and she left one brother back in Glasgow – Jack – who later married a woman called Lil and so we had cousins in Scotland, too.

My father had one brother, Larry, and two sisters, Josie and Agnes. Agnes married Jerry Farren, and both worked in Hills Department Store until they retired in their seventies. Agnes and Jerry didn't have any children. My father's only brother, Larry Hassan, was a big businessman in Derry and had five children with his wife, Nellie. He was perhaps best-known locally as owner of Austin's Department Store – one of the city's finest landmark buildings and the oldest department store in the world. However, Larry was also a world-renowned tenor singer who performed on BBC Radio and was among the first to sing on Radio Athlone in the 1930s.

My uncle Larry was one of the first people present to greet famous aviator Amelia Earhart when she landed her Lockheed Vega aeroplane in Gallagher's Field in May 1932. He's even in one of the photographs. By landing in Derry that day, Earhart became the first woman to fly solo across the Atlantic and earned her place in the history books. Larry was also a big golfing man and, while in America on a golf excursion once, he met Neil Armstrong – the first man on the moon. A framed photo of the two of them together was displayed in Austin's for decades afterwards.

Aunt Josie was a soprano singer who went to America to enhance her singing career. She sang in New York's Carnegie Hall and other prestigious venues. Josie met and married a New York businessman called Jim Donahue and stayed there, where they had a daughter, also called Josephine.

When he was a young man in July 1931, my father went out to America where he'd got a job as his sister's chauffeur! He basically had to drive Josie and her associates to various venues across New York where they were performing.

America at that time, and especially New York, could be quite a rough and dangerous place to work with prohibition still going on, which didn't end until 1933. But my father soon found he came in useful – as he knew how to make authentic Irish Poitín! A skill much sought after, I'm sure.

After a few years, Josie's husband died of a heart attack in Coney Island. A few months after Jim died, my father and his sister Josie and young Josie left America and returned home to Derry. On his return, my father got a job as a driver for McConnell's Tea Company in Foyle Street where he stayed for a few years, until eventually starting as a docker at Derry Port. Aunt Josie, meanwhile, leased out a house in Portstewart in the late 1930s and she turned it into a holiday boarding-house on the Promenade until retiring in the 1950s.

My grandfather, Dan Hassan, was a docker too, but after a bad accident at the quayside in the late 1930s, he had to give up dock-work. That's when my father got his docker badge, and he stayed on the docks until the Burns and Laird cross-channel shipping service was withdrawn from Derry port in the mid-1960s. It was so sad to see those big ships carrying passengers and general cargo between Derry to Glasgow being taken off service and never replaced. When the container service was later introduced, it finished off the cross-channel service for good.

My grandfather Hassan died in 1947, one year after I was born, so sadly I don't remember him. But I've been told so many stories about him over the years I've kept him in my memory throughout. Granny Hassan eventually went to live with Aunt Josie in Portstewart, where I remember her quite well as I spent many a happy time there staying with her.

As time went on, my father met my mother in 1940 and they were married in September 1943 at the Star of the Sea church in Portstewart. Their wedding reception was held in Aunt Josie's holiday house on the Promenade.

My parents were given the Papal Blessing by my mother's cousin Fr John O'Dowd O.F.M., who was assisted by Rev Hugh Conway Adm., Long Tower, Derry. Bridesmaid was Mary (Maisy) McLaughlin, a close friend of my mother's from Buncrana who was married to Neil Brennan and had three of a family. The best man was Paddy Hassan from Feeny village near Derry. Paddy was a close friend of the family who had spent time in the bar trade in both Belfast and America. He never married.

I was born on February 16, 1946 in Glasgow. My mother's father was extremely ill at the time she was expecting me, and she needed to go back over to Glasgow to look after him. While there, she gave birth to me in Maggie's family home at 476 Crown Street, where we stayed for a few months. My grandfather passed on after his short illness, and after the burial we returned to Derry and to our house in Bridge Street – our home until the new Carnhill estate in 1971.

As a family, we loved getting out of Derry to spend holidays at the farm in Terrydreen, where my father's people came from. My da loved the country and he loved getting to Mullaghash mountain to shoot rabbits and wild birds. In his younger days, he would slip away every other weekend to Mullaghash and other areas in the country to have a day's shooting.

I remember many times coming home from the country with pheasants and rabbits. I've already said that my mother was the best cook in Ireland and could make a dinner out of anything. Well, her rabbit stew was out of this world! I suppose people now would say, "Rabbit stew?!" But it was good. This went on for a few years until the rabbit's disease (myxomatosis) arrived, and that was the end of us bringing rabbits home.

The farm at Terrydreen was owned by the McCullough family, who were cousins of my father. There was Benny, Peter, Big Johnny, and Wee Mary, and they always made us very welcome. We loved going out working in the fields helping Benny and Peter gather in the hay. The Shamrock tea and scone bread that wee Mary brought to the field for us was something special, and I can almost taste it now.

We spent time in Buncrana and stayed at the castle, too. It was a creepy place, but we loved it. There was no electricity in the castle either, just oil lamps or candles, and it was always filled with people. It was such a big building that some of the biggest Boy Scouting movements around England and Scotland would come to Buncrana and stay for weeks. Another family who I recall staying were the Brennan family, as their relatives owned the Castle. As weans, we had a terrific time. Being so near the beach was brilliant, too, and we spent many hours there, as it was almost on castle grounds.

We would stay at the castle for two or three weeks, and I remember sitting on the bridge watching the salmon jumping in the Crana River. The castle had seen a lot of history over the years. When one of the founding members of the United Irishmen, Theobald Wolfe Tone, was captured by the British Navy in the Swilly in 1798, he was held at the castle before being taken on to Derry Jail.

There was always lots to do in Buncrana, like our morning visits to the neighbouring farm to get the milk for our cornflakes – milk straight from the cow! Washing ourselves at the Springwell to start the day, and even learning how to smoke in the old Cahir O'Doherty Keep, beside the river Crana, where 'Sweet Afton' was the order of the day.

Once during a spring tide, we went to Ned's Point, not far from the castle, to catch mackerel. We had no fishing rods, just a bucket! There were so many fish in the river you could just catch them in a bucket – this is true! When we went back to the castle with the mackerel, old Mrs McLaughlin cooked the fish on the big open fire, and I can still remember just how good that fish tasted.

On a few occasions we went to Portstewart for a week and had a wonderful time staying at Aunt Josie's house. The fun arcades were great for us as children, as was the massive beach at the strand. We had great times on these holidays.

As we got older, my brother Dessie would go with father for a day's shooting on the hill with his friends Johnny and Jimmy McFadden. Dessie, like our father, loved a bit of the country and the odd shot. They also did a lot of fishing in the river Fern and in the Faughan too. They spent many days fishing there, and Dessie would spend most of his holidays at the farm in Terrydreen.

I spent a lot of my holidays at Aunt Josie's in Portstewart, and sometimes a few weekends in the wintertime too. I loved the place, lying in bed at night listening to the waves crashing against the rocks was something special.

There would often be as many as twenty guests staying at Josie's holiday house at the promenade. I would run messages to the harbour for fresh fish just off the boat, or to the baker's shop for bread fresh from the oven, and things like that. I made friends with some of the people who came back for their holidays every year and there was always loads to do. Besides the fun arcades, there was a cinema along the promenade and the diving display from the herring pool above the harbour was great to watch. When the fun was over, we got to swim in the pool which was an experience I would never forget.

I have a vivid memory from when I was very young playing in Bridge Street. We were told about a fight at the Diamond, not far from our street, so a few of us ventured up into the town centre to see if we could see what was happening. When we got there, it looked like some kind of riot with hundreds of people and the RUC battling against what I now realise were protesters at the Diamond.

The RUC – Royal Ulster Constabulary – were the North's police force at that time, and their ranks were predominantly unionist.

I didn't understand at the time what this battle was all about, but I soon found out what the problem was. The Nationalist Party in the city had been trying to hold a St. Patrick's Day Parade. Marchers had left from the offices of the Derry Journal, which was in Shipquay Street back then, with the national flag held aloft to celebrate Ireland's patron saint, and the RUC were determined to stop them. I suppose this was the first time I'd witnessed political trouble on the streets of our city.

We had many nights of craic in our house in Bridge Street with get-togethers and sing-songs, and obviously Johnny Walker would be involved! Besides my mum and dad, sing-songs often featured our aunt Agnes, Jerry Farren, his brother Michael, and also their sister, May Farren, who played the piano. My da would sing The Old House, a John McCormick song, and Jerry Farren often sang the famous Irish ballad, The West's Awake. Agnes's favourite was always The Hills of Donegal, and May Farren would play all sorts of lovely tunes on the piano. Those were the days, or should I say, the nights.

They have now all gone, all these amazing people that we'll never forget. My mother was a hard-working woman who did a lot of dressmaking to put food on the table and keep the family safe. She was a brilliant seamstress and dressmaker and many people in the street came to her. Aunt Agnes was such a special person, she never forgot birthdays, Christmas, or holiday times and was always giving rather than taking. May they rest in peace.

Thinking back now though there is one thing I do regret. I wish I'd sat down with my father and asked him more about his time in America. I'd love to have known all about his experiences out there. I guess when you get older, you tend to think of things you should have done but didn't. He did tell us that he was once a cowboy though!

My Father died on September 8, 1979.

Mother died on October 3, 1998.

Aunt Agnes died in July 1979.

Uncle Jerry was murdered in his home at Hawkin Street for a £5 note in 1985.

Aunt Nelly died in July 1991.

Uncle Larry died at the age of 101 in August 2011.

Aunt Josie died in July 1981.

May Farren died on 15 March 1987, and their brother, Michael, in 1984.

CHAPTER 2
School Days

I started primary school in the early 1950s at about five years old. Luckily enough, I went to St Patrick's Boys' School at the top of Bridge Street, so it wasn't far to go in the mornings! Before that I had to do a year at Artillery Street school because there was no room at Bridge Street. Artillery Street was primarily for girls and run by the nuns, so I didn't like it much.

Although Bridge Street wasn't the best, the teachers were okay. One teacher there, Mr McBrearty, would shout so loud that people in the street would laugh hearing him from outside. When I'd go home at lunchtime, my mother told us she could hear him shouting from afar that morning.

One school friend I sat beside most of the time was Doggie McLaughlin. I kept in contact with Doggie for most of my life afterwards. He was an artist and could draw anything or anyone. He really should have made a fortune.

I remember Father Rooney coming in and questioning the class on the Catechism. It was in Religious Examination, where we had to stand around the back of the room to answer questions. If we were right, we got an apple. If we were wrong, we got the cane. Every October, the school made us go to October devotions at three o'clock, marching the whole school up to the Long Tower chapel past the Derry Walls and Long Tower Street. Inevitably, some of the class dropped out on the way and sneaked away home. They were never missed. The school's head, Mr Hutton, was extremely strict but a gentleman also. Another young trainee teacher, Don Doherty, was great to work with because he was a most modern type of teacher. We liked him a lot. He also remembered us when we met him years afterwards. Mr Doherty was a superb snooker player in the city, so from time to time we would run into him in the snooker venues.

Boys from St Joseph's Home in Termonbacca also attended the Bridge Street school alongside us. Termonbacca was run by the authoritarian Sisters of Nazareth. Little did we know back then just how badly these boys were being treated in these homes. There has been a huge inquiry since, the Historical Abuse Inquiry. When we were at school, some of these boys from the home would make friends with families in the street. A few families would invite the boys in and give them some lunch, my mother included. She made sure one of these boys ate lunch every day, and it lasted for a while – until the nuns found out and stopped it. As a result of people feeding them, the boys weren't allowed out at lunchtime anymore, and had to stay in the school playground.

We had good times at that school, but they didn't last forever and sometime around 1956 we were told that St Patrick's might be closing. My mother was told she had to find another school for me and my brother, and she tried a few schools at the time, but they were all full up. The only school we could get into was the Waterside Boy's School at Chapel Road. But of course, as soon as we started there, we were told that the Bridge Street School had been given a reprieve. In the end, it didn't close until the late 1960s, and it was finally demolished in the early 1990s to make way for Foyleside Shopping Centre.

Waterside Boys' School was a far more modern school and completely different from St Patrick's. The headmaster was extremely strict on timekeeping, but thankfully the school wasn't too far away, and we braved the elements in the brisk walk over Craigavon Bridge. One thing I remember about going to school was that both ends of the bridge had sandbag posts with police inside and guns pointing out at you. I thought this was funny and I don't think I understood why at the time. I was only eleven or so. Obviously, we had no idea of the years and decades ahead.

This was a big school with a canteen separate from the school building, which was quite unusual in Derry at that time. I remember that Mr Friel, the music teacher, was very strict, but that Mr Joe McCourt was a fair and good teacher, as was Mr Day. As I recall, Mr Day was also in the Knights of Malta, a voluntary first aid organisation active at the time, and was very down to earth with the class. Mr Day had a nickname, Tusa, and he was a good spud. Because we were in the leaving class with Mr Day, we got to do things like helping the canteen staff or assisting with gardening and keeping the footpaths clean.

One of the places we played in growing up was the old opera house in Carlisle Road, which was derelict after being burned to the ground in 1944. Some say it was the IRA who were responsible for the fire, because the opera house was showing British propaganda films. It was left in a bad state.

We would get into the opera house through the backyard of the Ryan family's house, climbing over the wall to get into the building. In hindsight, it was such a dangerous place for youngsters to play, but we thought it was brilliant being able to walk across the bare steel frames that once supported floors and to explore the ruins.

Coming up to August 12th every year, our Bridge Street gang would raid the bonfire material in the Fountain and take it to where we had our own August

15th bonfire! Then the Fountain gang would come in the middle of the night to raid our site and take back their material, but it was all in good spirit.

Some Sundays we would go down to the quay to see all the Navy ships that were stationed or docked under NATO, with Canadians, Portuguese, Norwegians, British, and Americans ships. People were allowed on the ships with a guide, and the American vessels were always the best because they were so friendly and gave us bottles of Coca-Cola and American cigarettes.

In the summer, some of us would dob off school and go to Kilfennan to gather spuds for the local farmer. I did it once, but others carried on until they were all caught. I never liked school really. I feel like I didn't learn much. I know they say that school days are the best days, and for some that might be true, but in my case, learning started after I left school and entered the university of life.

After school, the gang would play football or marbles there was Dessie, Pasty Donnelly, Ray and Eddy Ryan, Seamus and big Willie McCourt Michael and Danny O'Connor, Bernard and Johnny McMonagle, 'Maker', Tony Smith, Joe and Micky Doherty, John and Michael Gallagher, and Richard Devenney to name but a few. Of course, I must name some of the girls I remember back then, like Mary and Vicky Brown, Ann Carlin, Sadie Gallagher, Deborah McSherrie and Mary McCourt, and lots of others besides.

We had a football team in the street, and we travelled to different parts of the city to play in Meenan Park, and Iona Park, which was the landfill site for the council. Iona Park was a lovely development, as I recall, and we played a big match there on the opening night.

I remember one time that the gang and I were "acting the maggot" in the street, as our parents would say, and a window was broken. I got the blame for breaking it, so the woman who lived in the house marched down to our house to tell my da that I broke her window!

When I got home later, I got a slap with no questions asked! A few hours later the woman came back to tell my da that it wasn't me and she'd found the culprit. The motto of that story is that whether you did it or didn't do it, you still got a slap for it. How times change, as my son would not react the same way nowadays at all!

The Bridge Street community was predominantly nationalist, and the older people in the street told us stories about the 1920s when conflict erupted in the city. Granny Hassan said that, at the time, they weren't allowed to leave their homes because of the curfews and risked being shot if they did. Enforcing the curfews were the Queen's and Dorset regiments, and they did shoot several Catholics.

Granny told us about a man called Barney Doyle, who was on the run from the Brits in the 1920s. No wonder they couldn't find him – my granny hid him underneath the coal in our cellar! Doyle's mother, who lived across the street from our house, would stand at her front door armed with a sweeping brush waiting for the Brits who dared to come up the street.

We were told many stories of what happened at that time in Derry. The Corporation had the city's first Catholic majority in the Council in 1920, and there was its first nationalist mayor, Hugh O'Doherty.

The grandfathers of two of our party's esteemed members, Bobby Kelly R.I.P. and Raymond McCartney, were also in that corporation (Robert McAnaney and James Gallagher). Isn't it interesting how history repeats through generations? Elected that year 1920 were ten Sinn Féin councillors and ten nationalists. Some couldn't use the name Sinn Féin at the time because they would have been arrested for it. The unionists had nineteen members in the Corporation.

What's known today as 'The Derry Riots' took place in June 1920 and lasted a week, with confrontations between the city's unionists and nationalists reaching boiling point. This conflict ended in the deaths of twenty nationalist civilians. I remember my granny telling us that two of those killed were shot at the bottom of Bridge Street, and that their bodies lay there in the street for two days as people were too afraid to leave their homes.

It is only since the recent 1916 anniversaries that we, as a population, have started to question and reflect on the events of 1920 in Derry and their wider historical relevance.

My opinion on 1916 and the War of Independence is that if Michael Collins had lived, Ireland would have been freed long ago. Collins would have found a way to reunite the country.

I feel that unionist politicians in the North – and the communities they represent – have never really understood why many nationalists and republicans feel unable to support or celebrate the 100-year centenary of its so-called Northern Ireland state. They don't seem to realise the significance of 1921 Partition of Ireland, and how it separated our country indefinitely. How can we, after fifty years of very deliberate misrule and the claim of a Protestant state for a Protestant people, celebrate this partition and its effects?

These policies ensured decades of unionist discrimination and domination across the north of Ireland. The vast majority of Catholics across the North had no voting rights and no real voice to affect meaningful change.

In Derry, particularly, the gerrymandered electoral areas succeeded in keeping all its Catholic citizens in their place, in their area and largely unrepresented in local and regional government. Coupled with this was notoriously-bad housing in Derry and across the North, and widespread neglect and negation of its Catholic population. Half a century of neglect had created a need for more. We demanded more.

I strongly feel that because of this illegal state, citizens across the North were forced into the events that followed. There is a good reason why we don't - and we shouldn't – ever understand the partition of our country.

CHAPTER 3
GROWING UP IN BRIDGE STREET

I have so many memories of our childhood in Bridge Street, a real adventure playground for us in those days. We had our pick of streets and back alleys to explore, as far as Sugarhouse Lane, Matty's Lane, Orchard Lane and the Battery, and also near the old Opera House and as far down as Derry quay. These lands encompassed our whole lives. We played football at Sugarhouse Lane, and sometimes at Foyle Road beside the G.N.R. railway station.

Bridge Street - so-named because it once led to the original wooden Derry Bridge – was filled with community, craic and memorable characters. We had four shops in the street, including Johnny Kilkie's, Maggie Doherty's and McSherrie's. On the corner of Bridge Street and Foyle Street was Tommy Williams's Shoe Shop, where my aunt Agnes had bought me my First Communion shoes as a boy. Nowadays, shoes are considered expendable but back then we never threw shoes out – we had everything repaired and the shoemaker would make them good as new again. I remember many times going to Freddie Clifford's repair shop in Linenhall Street and, later, to Abercorn Road after Freddie relocated his shop to make way for the Richmond Centre development.

When I was young, Bridge Street had a number of pubs and bars dotted along it, including the Oregon Bar, The Star, the American Bar, McGinley's Bar, which was called 'the bucket of blood', McIntyre's and John Eddie's, which was better known as the Capstan Bar. That was at the very top of Bridge Street adjoining Orchard Street.

I still recall many of those who lived around us. Kathleen, Micky, and Phonsie Kelly lived in the only house in Foyle Alley, a tiny laneway that led to Foyle Street. There was also a cooperage or cooper's yard that made wooden barrels probably for the drink industry. Joe Bradley's barber shop was at the bottom of Bridge Street beside Hunter's Bakery. Joe ran it with his brother, Phil, and Joe would cut hair with a cigarette in his mouth, more ash than hair falling over you! If we needed a haircut, we got the haircut on a Monday and Joe was paid on a Friday and that was just the way it was. Joe got a lot of passing trade from the buses for Donegal that parked at the G.N.R. Station in Foyle Road. The Oregon Bar, which later became the Hayloft, was one of the first singing bars in the city and only about three doors away from our house. I remember how, as weans, we would lie in bed at night listening to all the singing and craic from the bar.

I'll never forget the evening when our wee Bridge Street gang were all playing marbles at what we called the Battery in our street. There we were, and all of a sudden, the whole gable wall of McIntyre's Pub gable gave way and fell into the Battery! We could see all the people standing at the bar counter, still drinking – that's how fast it happened. It's a miracle that no-one was killed. Because of the collapse, the rest of the building was deemed unsafe and eventually had to be knocked down.

After that happened, a lot of people in our area began to question the condition of their own homes, concerned about the integrity and safety of these old dwellings. Most of our street was in a terrible condition, and it was a disgrace so many families were forced to live there, sometimes several to a house.

Despite their woes, people tended to get on with their lives and make the best of their situation. My family and many others in Bridge Street depended on support from the dole and National Assistance because there was no work in the city. My father would get two or three day's work at the docks, and on the other days he would sign on the dole. If the dole couldn't help, people had to go to Ivy House, the National Assistance office on the Strand Road, which was a very degrading place that didn't treat people very well at all.

There were some great characters in Bridge Street, like big Heavy McAllister and Annie Green. Annie lived in Millers Close where about five or six families also lived, Annie was known to smuggle butter over the border for people in the street - including my ma. Once the RUC got suspicious about Annie and they followed her coming off the train from Carrigans and heading straight towards our house, laden with contraband items smuggled in for others. The RUC officer came to our door, insisting they'd seen her go in and threatening to come inside and pull up every floorboard looking for her if my mother didn't hand her over. Of course, my ma wasn't having any of this and told that RUC man where to go!

In the late fifties there was a bread strike across the North, so our gang got a lend of a trolley and went out to Killea – just over the border – to bring bread back for the street. I think the strike lasted a week or so and we took turns to get the bread for everyone.

Maggie McKay would come down the street to the train station and raise murder, shouting and cursing at everybody that looked in her direction. Then there was Paddy and Maggie Long, who I remember always sitting on someone's doorstep smoking a clay pipe. We were afraid of them in a way, but if they shouted anything, some of the gang would shout back.

Dickie and Joey Valley lived in the street, too, and they were good craic. Dickie was a great swimmer and often swam across the Foyle. Sometimes Dickie and Joey would don their boxing gloves and put on a show of boxing in the street, and poor Joey often got the worst of the fight. It was all good fun though.

Bridge Street also had some bare-knuckle street fights in its time, too. When we were younger, my brother and I would watch from the upstairs window as the fights took place outside. It was reminiscent of the fight scene in the film, The Quiet Man, when Sean Thornton and Squire Red Will Danaher fought it out over Mary Kate Danaher. In Bridge Street, opponents ended up shaking hands with their disputes sorted.

My granny told us the story about the 1943 great escape from Derry Jail when republicans tunnelled their way out of the jail and into the backyard of a family's home in Harding Street! Only to be recaptured and interned in Donegal. Our history is full of such stories.

When I was about eleven, I remember seeing Johnny McBride's pipe band coming down Bridge Street led by the national flag and playing A Nation Once Again, an old 19th Century song about independence from Britain. That day we followed the band the whole way down the street, and at the bottom of the street between the junction of Foyle Street and John Street, the RUC were waiting to arrest everyone! The whole band was put into the RUC's big black tender vans and taken to Victoria Barracks. It blew over, of course, and they continued performing for years despite intermittent RUC visits. They persevered, and later became the Pearse Brothers' Pipe Band and, after that, the Colmcille Pipe Band who were run by a Hasson family in Shantallow (no relation of ours).

Long before the days of brown recycling food-bins, a woman called Nelly Stewart kept pigs in her Bridge Street backyard. The whole street's daily scraps and leftovers of course went to her pigs.

Almost in direct contrast to Nelly's piggy haven that we fed with scraps, we also lived near the pork factory and experienced a whole different side of things.

In those days, Biggers's Pork Store had its front entrance in Foyle Street and its back entrance opening onto Bridge Street at the Battery beside Bernard McMonagle house.

Every three days or so, the UTA transport lorries loaded with pigs would come up our street to offload the pigs into the slaughterhouse or abattoir. As they were waiting to discharge their pigs, lorries would often line up in the street waiting their turn. In hindsight, the dirt, water and effluent from these pigs would literally flow down our street and the smell would be truly awful. That kind of thing would never be allowed to happen now with modern health and safety concerns, but in those days, people got away with things like that, with not a word said. One of the things I remember most about those times is that, because we did not live far from the slaughterhouse, we could hear the pigs scream in terror at night as they were being killed. I can still remember it. This would never happen nowadays. Across from Bigger's Pork Store was Buchanan's Pork Store – so we couldn't escape it.

Alongside these we had Brown's Foundry, which was in Foyle Street. We also had the shirt factory and several bars, including the Mourne Bar, Breslin's Bar, which was called the Tavern, and the Sailor's Rest across from Christy's Grain Mill. Then there was Willie Irvine's paper shop, where you got any magazines you wanted, along with sweets and all kinds of tobacco. Next door to that was the weights and measure shop. The Burke family lived next door to Mrs Conwell's Cafe and Ice Cream Parlour, and then Bridget Mailey's Public House and Dalton's Bar existed alongside each other.

We were lucky enough to live around a few involved in the showband era, too. These included Barney Coyle, who lived in our street, and the Lindsay Family. We could always hear Noel Lindsay practising on his trumpet as we passed by his house. There was also the Brown family, the McShanes, and Micky (Mike) McGeady, who played the sax, and was part of the Big Four Showband with Pat McGuigan, father of the champion boxer Barry McGuigan.

All these musicians learned their trade in the St Columb's T.A. band that, at the time, had its base in St. Columb's Minor Hall in Orchard Street. A family friend, Micky McGeady, played in the band back then and asked me to join up. I was about thirteen at the time and agreed to join the band. They gave me the French Horn, which I didn't particularly like and so I left the band after three months.

Not many families in Bridge Street had a television in the 1950s, and our house didn't get one until the late '50s at least. Before that we would go up the town and watch TV through the shop windows, usually at Cavendish's big shop in Bishop Street. That was the place to go.

The family of one of our gang, Danny O'Connor, had a television before the rest of us, and he would let us watch the football matches in his house. That was the first time I watched a proper match on telly, seeing Manchester United playing Real Madrid around 1956 or 1957.

We often played around the quay in those days because Bridge Street was not very far from the riverfront. In hindsight, it must have been a very dangerous area for children to play, but we thought it was great. When young, you are sometimes oblivious to the dangers.

We also played in Christy's Grain Mill in Foyle Street. Sometimes the rats were as big as cats, but it never deterred us from sneaking into Christy's Mill to get some grain when trying to catch pigeons. We did this so many times, until one time, when about four of us went in to get some grain. As we were lifting the grain, out jumped what we thought was a rat! In fact, it was a mongoose that Christy's Mill kept around to kill rats and keep intruders at bay! Well, that was the last time I went into that mill. It wasn't worth facing the mongoose!

In those days, most of the things one needed were sold by people coming around the street and our house was no different. I remember the buttermilk man with his horse and cart, coming around selling buttermilk. My mother would give me a jug and send me out - and he would fill it up for one shilling. It was lovely to drink, but Maggie would use it for baking instead.

On Fridays we would get the "fresh herring" call in the street from another wee man and his hand cart. Then there was Johnny the milkman, who was from the country but delivered the milk every day to our whole neighbourhood and more. Johnny would sometimes get his tea break in our house, and I remember that when he retired, big Johnny Traynor, from Creggan, took over his run. Those were the days when you could expect the daily delivery of milk, cream, and bottles of orange drinks.

On Saturday mornings, my mother would often ask me to go to the Slate Club in St, Columb's Hall in Orchard Street. This was a savings account of some kind, and she would send me to pay in money that became savings that she could lift at Christmas time. In those days, there was no such thing as the Credit Union, and it was through ideas like this that our parents got help. The people of Derry used the Slate Club to have a bit of money at Christmas, paying in what they could afford each week and withdrawing it when Christmas came around.

One of our treats as children was when my da would take me and my younger brother up to the Long Tower Christmas Funfair at Bishop Street. It was great to win a box of biscuits or chocolates and other prizes at the rickety wheel. In those days, winning a box of sweets or biscuits would be a real buzz, but nowadays they're available anytime.

Micky McGeady and his mother were great friends of our family, and they lived in a particularly run-down part of Bridge Street that we all called "The Castle". The building itself was in a bad state with five or six families crammed into it awaiting relocation. Thankfully, it was among the first buildings addressed during the redevelopment of the street.

The redevelopment was good news because it sought to get rid of most of the really bad housing, but the community was less enthused about the idea. About a quarter of the houses on our street were knocked down, with residents forced to find elsewhere to live. Most went to new homes in Bluebell Hill Gardens in the nearby Brandywell area, while others went to Creggan or to Shantallow, a newer estate on the outskirts of the city.

When some of our friends moved to Bluebell Gardens in the Brandywell area, a few of us would still go over to them. We all joined the youth club in Our Lady of Lourdes Hall in the Brandywell, and it was great as there was always lots to do, including going to the pictures on a Sunday evening and a hop [dance] at night.

We had so many friends and acquaintances over the years in Bridge Street. One good friend of our family was Johnny Kilkie, whom I respected very much, and who had a shop across the street from us. I remember how I would spend hours just standing in his shop, talking about a range of things from politics and religion or anything else that came up. If I had a problem, I felt I could talk to Johnny and get his advice. He was a fisherman who loved nothing more than getting on his racer bike on a Sunday morning and getting out of the city to spend the whole day fishing. If he caught some fish, he would send some over to my mother.

One of the saddest days I recall from growing up in Bridge Street was when Patsy Donnelly's sister, Peggy, was knocked down and killed by a lorry. We were all playing together in the street when Peggy ran out onto the road and was hit. It was such a terrible day in Bridge Street, and I think that Peggy's parents, Lizzie and Paddy, never got over her death. That's actually something I will never forget. There was so much sadness in the street for a long time afterwards.

When the council announced major redevelopment plans of our area to build Foyleside Shopping Centre in the early 1990s, we knew it was high time. Most of Bridge Street and all of Sugarhouse Lane, Matty's Lane, Orchard Lane and Orchard Street were demolished to make way for the new shopping centre. A substantial section of Foyle Street was demolished too. It was difficult, I suppose this is progress as our city evolves and develops. In all, around 200 families were rehoused all over the city, including to the Waterside. When that happened, we missed Bridge Street. It was our place and our playground.

A lot of local businesses were affected by the redevelopment, too, like the Wembley Fish and Chip Shop at the top of Orchard Street. Then there were the trade union rooms and offices that were affected, as was the Belfast Telegraph office, the bookies and the Atlantic Bar at the bottom of Orchard Street. In fact, Badger's Pub is the only building left in Orchard Street nowadays. Back then, it used to be called McGirrs, then it became Dalton's public house and finally, Badgers. It's still going strong.

Back then, we had the Melville Hotel at Foyle Street – a beautiful Art Deco hotel that had all the big-bands and showbands of its day. It was beside Mortimer's Chemist, and I remember there was a big fire at the Melville Hotel that tragically killed two firemen. The chemists building had a lot of flammable materials that worried everyone that night too.

Where our house once stood in Bridge Street eventually became the Metropole sheltered housing building, which was owned by Choice Housing Association. The Metropole takes its name from the Metropole Hotel that was on the same site in the 1950s, which it replaced. The funny thing was their address is the same as the address of our house, 55 Bridge Street.

Years later, as an elected representative of Derry City Council, I remember that we had a meeting with one of our fellow councillors, Billy Page, about Choice Housing's proposals for the city at that time. We were strict in what we needed. I recall that during that meeting, I told the Choice Housing representative that the very room we were sitting in that day could have been our family's living room - number 55. Our house would have roughly occupied the same site. The area that we lived in also included Davey McClain's timber yard, which was wedged in between Johnny Kilkie's shop, Big Willie's and Seamus McCourt's family homes, not forgetting St, Patrick's Boys' School, which was brought into this massive development of the area. From then on, people from Bridge Street were given new homes all over the city, and I'm quietly confident that no matter where people were from, they had historic links to Bridge Street somehow.

One thing that did disappoint me was that this historical part of Derry had become very much overlooked in the years since. The Foyleside development took over everything for a while – including our childhood stories. I feel more should have been made of these historical connections at the time.

CHAPTER 4
Working Days

When I left school around Easter time in 1960, my first job was as a message boy in Harry Doherty's shop in Creggan. For the sum of £1.50 per week, I had to deliver groceries in and around the Creggan area and I loved it. It was a great job, and the shop was always full of people. I met so many interesting folk in the six months I worked there, and I learned so much about life. If I wasn't delivering groceries, then I was bagging spuds or serving in the shop itself.

I remember once delivering groceries in the middle of what we called Hurricane Debbie. I was blown totally off the bike by the winds, and all the groceries I was supposed to be delivering were thrown all over the place too. That was an experience! On the whole, Harry Doherty was well known for doing a lot of good work ensuring the people of Creggan and beyond had what they needed to survive. He was a massive sports-fan too and a boxing promoter for a time.

When I left Harry Doherty's shop, I got an interview for the Birmingham Sound Reproducers (BSR) Factory in Derry's Bligh's Lane. At that time, the BSR was one of the major employers for men in the city and its factory made parts for record players.

I started in the BSR Factory in November 1961, and I felt this was a job to be proud of. My first wage with them was £2.60 per week back then, which rose to nearly £4.00 per week if we worked overtime.

We worked on the conveyor belt, putting the motors on the record players. It was a job we were expected to be speedy at, and it was often hard to fathom. My sidekick on the opposite side of the belt was Joe Doherty, a fellow Bridge Street native, and he often helped me keep pace with the workload. Another friend worked there, too - Danny Crerand. He was actually an inspector for the factory.

While I was at the BSR, there were several serious disputes to deal with, and two pay-offs within the company. I was given redundancy in the first wave of pay-offs but was later brought back after three months.

After that, the factory introduced a new tape recorder in the system and required staff to work the lines again. I agreed to work the line, putting the motors on the new record-playing machines, and my sidekick at that time was a man called Colum Norris.

The factory finally closed its doors in 1967, putting almost 2,000 people out of work across the city of Derry and devastating the male workforce. That was such a sad time for Derry, with so many men women and boys forced to claim the dole at the time just to make ends meet.

After the BSR, I was out of work for around a month when we heard that a new factory was coming to Derry, and it needed volunteers to go over to England to train. I inquired at the dole office in Derry and got an interview for one of these new positions.

The new job was at the LEC Refrigeration Company, who had built a new factory at Maydown, but were originally based at Bognor Regis in England. In total, twenty-two Derry trainees were flown to England for training. We were each told that the conditions and wages of this new job were exceptionally good, which we were pleased about to be honest. Management put us all up for two weeks in a Butlin's holiday camp, until they managed to get accommodation for us all in England. The company, LEC, made fridges and fridge freezers and their new factory was nearing completion in Derry.

As we trained up in England, we were informed that the factory in Derry was almost completed. I was trained in bench-fitting and drilling, and the working conditions were not bad. The wages were better than the BSR, too, and with a bit of overtime we heard that workers could earn as much as £35 a week.

I worked there for five months until August 1968, when I went back to Derry. I arrived back on 12 August 1968, and after getting home I met some friends who told me about another new factory in Maydown, Towler Hydraulics, who were looking for bench-fitters.

The next morning, I went down to this new factory and asked to see someone. A man called Stan Pye came out and introduced himself as Foreman of the plant, and I told him that I was looking for a job and had just come back from working in England. After a brief discussion, he asked when I could start, and I said now - so I got the job.

Towler Hydraulics specialised in the manufacture of high-pressure oil hydraulic pumps for the oil industry, and they were looking for bench-fitters and drillers. They had two shift policies in the factory, and Towlers operated on piecework, which means you were paid based on how much work you did. It was the best job I ever had, and the conditions were great. The money was very good, too, and you could earn £80 or 90 in your hand a week if you were lucky. If your workload was not finished, you were paid a percentage of what was done when the job was finished and the rest as a bonus.

Sadly, that factory was affected by the same saga that always hits Derry. The factory ran into difficulty and began paying people off, including me. In 1972, the Derry factory eventually closed, and operations went back to its parent factory in Leeds. After Towlers, I got a job at Regna International in Springtown industrial Estate. They made cash registers, and I worked there for two years until 1974, assembling parts for the cash registers.

From then on, I was unemployed for three months and a friend of mine, Davey Collins, asked me to give him a lift down to Maydown for an interview in Hutchinson Yarn Factory (Courtaulds Group). Of course, I drove him down to the factory and waited for him while he went for his job interview. I knew the personnel manager at this factory, Eamon Nolan, and I had asked Davey to tell Eamon that I was looking for a job.

While I sat there in the car at the gate house for Davey to finish his interview, Eamon Nolan called the gate-man and told him to send me up for an interview, too. He offered me a job in the warehouse, starting the next day. I accepted.

The job consisted of loading heavy, forty-foot containers and then stacking the boxes of yarn as they came off the conveyor belt into pallets. The craic was great, and the Foreman, Jerry Sharkey, had worked with us previously in the BSR Factory. We worked with such a great bunch of lads, including the O'Brien brothers, big John Traynor, John Nash, Danny Gallagher and Leo Macari. Looking back, I have to say that I looked forward to going to work in those days. Leo was a brilliant colleague to work with, as were all the others.

Like so many other factories in Derry over the years, Hutchinson Yarn Factory eventually ran into difficulty and closed its doors in November 1979. Once again, I was out of a job and unsure of which direction to take next. Jobs were scarce, and though I applied to several, I got nowhere. Perhaps because I was a member of Sinn Féin. I applied for several jobs unsuccessfully, and it was around then that I decided to work full-time for the party.

CHAPTER 5
THE SIXTIES

The 1960s were a great time to be alive, and people from my generation often say now that if you didn't live through the 1960s, you didn't truly live!

While people here struggled to kick-start the civil rights campaign, we looked to international events as our inspiration. We had JFK, The Beatles and the moon-landings making headlines globally. In the North, we revelled in bands like The Miami Showband, Joe Dolan and The Drifters, The Woodchoppers, with Dickie McManus, and Willy Bradley. We danced at long-forgotten dance-halls all over the place, including Borderland, the Plaza, the Corinthian, the Orchid in Lifford, and Derry's Guildhall as well.

Among the best of the dance halls were two venues straddling the border between North and South just outside Derry, the Plaza in Buncrana, Co. Donegal, and Borderland on the border of Derry and Muff, also in Co. Donegal, which often had the best bands around. In the summertime particularly, they would book all the most popular showbands and we loved it.

Buncrana's Plaza was later destroyed by fire, which was terrible, and we all broke our hearts when we heard about it. I hope the relevant authorities in Buncrana, or Donegal Council, restore the building to its former glory. The Plaza was majestic in its day and became meaningful to so many over the years.

Sometimes we went to mid-week gigs at the Plaza or Borderland when the bigger showbands were on. On more than a few occasions, we missed our bus home from Buncrana after a night's dancing to the Miami Showband, and we had to walk most of the way to Derry! We usually had to start work the next day at 8am, but we still did it – and it was worth it.

At the time, most people our age and above followed the Miami Showband with Dickie Rock. He was the star attraction and very popular with the fans, ensuring a packed audience at every performance. We often joked that we went to the Miami Showband gigs for the talent [attractive people] they attracted, rather than the music itself!

The universal appeal of our Irish showbands changed forever after 31 July 1975, when the Miami Showband were attacked on their way home from a gig Posing as a fake British army patrol, members of the Ulster Defence Regiment (UDR) and Ulster Volunteer Force (UVF) boarded the band's minibus and attempted to plant explosives to discredit the vehicles occupants. The bomb exploded prematurely, killing two of the attackers, Harris Boyle and Wesley Somerville. The gang then opened fire on band members themselves, murdering lead singer Fran O'Toole, guitarist Tony Geraghty and trumpeter Brian McCoy. They also injured two other band members, Des McAlea and Stephen Travers, who thankfully survived. The Miami Showband Massacre was a devastatingly sad time, not only for the band's families, but for the country as a whole. The Miami Showband were loved by so many people of my generation - we just couldn't understand why this had happened to them.

We still loved the dances. That didn't change. How could we forget Billy Tyson and the Esquires showband, bouncing all over the stage at the Corinthian Ballroom? Or Jumping Johnny Lee? Those were the days. When we went to the dances, we made new friends like Packie Gillespie, Lorny McIvor, John Millar, Eamonn Brady, John Hutton, Anthony Tyson, Mickey Doherty, and others.

I remember a night at the Cameo Ballroom, which once stood on Abbey Street in the Bogside, where the Derry Credit Union is now. One night a visiting band started to play God Save the Queen, and there was quite a commotion from the audience there! The band only stopped playing it when it was made clear that they were in the wrong place and at the wrong time to comfortably play such a tune!

As friends, we all planned our holidays together in the early 1960s. We went to Bray and Dublin in 1963, and were joined by John Gibbons, Barney Kelly and Bernard McMonagle. The following year, 1964, saw us going to Butlins at Mosney for a week – our first time there. That was fantastic, and we were joined by Tommy O'Kane, Billy McCauley and of course people from my own wee gang, Miller, Hutton, McIvor, and Packy. The craic was ninety that year!

The following year – 1965 – I didn't go on holiday as I had just passed my driving test. Instead, I went to the Credit Union and got a loan to buy my first car for £74. It was a blue Ford 100E type. I got a good deal on the car because my mother's relatives in Scotland had a car showroom that dealt in new and used cars. I vividly recall standing at the Derry quay, waiting for what we called the Scotch Boat to arrive with my new car, and watching as the car was taken off the boat. I felt so proud - my first car. Instead of wasting money on holidays, I spent that whole summer driving here, there and everywhere. At that time, I was still working in the BSR Factory, and it was so handy to get into the car in the mornings and drive to work. It was also brilliant being able to drive to the dances instead of waiting for buses for Borderland and the Plaza.

My father was still working at the Derry docks around then, and sometimes I would get a job at the Scotch Boat on a Saturday, which was well worth it. My wages in the BSR at the time, including overtime, worked out around £7 per week, whereas at the docks I could earn as much as £12/£15 per day for an 8am-2pm shift.

In 1966, the World Cup year, all the gang went to Butlins again for a week and had a ball. Some of us then went to Bray for another week. Those were great times, the 1960s were really buzzing.

Father Daly's concerts in St Columb's Hall every Sunday night were always packed to capacity with famous stars like Chubby Checker, Jim Reeves, The Bachelors and, of course, Frank Carson, whom I think actually started his career at St Columb's Hall. We looked forward to Sundays and seeing who would be performing each night. The proceeds of these concerts went to the Catholic Building Fund.

When US President John F Kennedy was assassinated in 1963, Father Daly put on a specific tribute to him at one of his concerts in St Columb's Hall, and I remember that we could have heard a pin drop in the hall as he paid tribute. The death of Kennedy hit us all hard, and I still remember where I was the night JFK was assassinated – as I'm sure many others do. That night I was at the Strand Picture House, and news of the assassination came up on the screen during the film we were watching.

Earlier, during the 1950s, St Columb's Hall was used as a chapel for women's and men's week-long religious retreats. I attended retreats there myself from the age of eleven with my brother and da, and when the retreat was over, the place always transformed back into a picture house with a free film for everybody that could get a ticket.

My parents were deeply religious and very devout Catholics. My father went to Lough Derg every spring with his friends Charlie Gallagher, Paddy Harkin, and a few others. There were five of them altogether, and they never missed a year at Lough Derg. My daddy would always bring us back some bars of rock from there too, which we always looked forward to.

Unless we went dancing, we'd meet up on Saturday nights at Deehan's Bar on Dungiven Road, where the craic was always good and a fair few songs were rendered. My mate McIvor would always sing the same song, The Rose of Tralee, and we would all sing along. The bar was mixed with both Catholics and Protestants, and everyone got along with one another with no problems.

Sometimes, Deehan's Bar ran a bus-outing to Donegal and the bus was always packed and we would have the greatest time away for the day. On Monday nights, we often played darts in the Strand Bar, and again, the craic was always good. John Miller and John Hutton were always the best at darts, and in fact, I think the rest of us were so bad it made the two John's look good! Going home, we'd go into Maggie Friel's fish shop for a plate of chips on her famous tin plates. I can still taste the chips, they were lovely.

Our friend, Packie Gillespie, was a baker who worked in the West End Bakery on the Lecky Road, beside Stephen Morgan's rags store and the big house where the Carlin's lived. I remember how we'd call into the bakery on our way from the midnight cinema at Strand Picture House, and Packie would give us warm baps and sausage rolls just out of the oven.

In the 1960s, Derry had six picture houses, or cinemas, as you would call them now. We had the Strand/Odeon, a beautiful Art Deco building on Strand Road, the Rialto/ABC on Newmarket Street, the Palace, which was situated where the River Inn and Silver Street is today, and the City Picture House in William Street, on the edge of the Bogside. If we missed the picture at the Strand, we could run across the bridge and catch the film again at The Midland picture house in the Waterside. They're all long gone now.

* * *

Derry City F.C. was a great team in the 1960s, winning the Irish Cup, the Football League and the Gold Cup thanks to players like Dougie Wood, Matt Doherty, Eddie Mahon and Jimbo Crossan, as well as Joe Wilson and Jimmy McGeough. Every week, the Brandywell was filled to capacity and City was getting the biggest games in the League at that time. We looked forward to every home game in the Brandywell.

In 1964, Derry beat Glentoran in the Irish Cup, and all the gang travelled up to Belfast to watch the game. After the match, we went into Belfast city centre to get something to eat and as we were walking around, we were stopped by the RUC and told to take off our Derry scarves and badges in case we caused offence to people in the shopping area! I think this was the start of my own personal realisation that something wasn't right in the North when a football scarf and badge could be considered offensive.

Those years were golden for Derry City. For the first time in European Football, we were well-beaten by Steaua Bucharest. Say no more. We also could never forget the game against FK Lyn Oslo, and the wonder goal scored by Jimbo Crossan on that wet, windy night to remember. In 1965, the same month that City won the Irish League, the Candy Stripes also took on a Spanish select team in Madrid who were preparing for a World Cup. Derry City lost 3-1.

The big debate among Derry City fans over the last thirty years is, of course, which team was the best - Derry in the 1960s or Jim McLaughlin's team that won the treble in the 1980s. The 1960s team had some powerful players, and I can't help but think that if Jim McLaughlin had some of those players on his team alongside some of his 1980s players, he would have won many more trebles.

Derry City Football Club had to leave the Irish League because of trouble that occurred back then. A bus bringing Ballymena players to Derry was hijacked and burned out, and after that happened, it was years before football came back to the Brandywell.

Almost thirteen more years passed before Derry City joined the League of Ireland, and that was the best thing that ever happened to them. When Derry was allowed into the League of Ireland during the 1985/86 season, huge crowds attended the games, and it was a great time for the city. Matches were something we looked forward to each week, and we couldn't wait until the next Sunday's home game to see players like Owen da Gama, Nelson Da Silva, Felix Healy and Noel King take to the pitch.

When I had children of my own, I'd take both Ciarán and Áine over to the Brandywell every week for Derry City matches. They looked forward to the matches just as much as I did, and we'd have two lemonade crates and a long wooden plank in the boot of my car to create the perfect Grandstand view. Another good friend of mine, Robbie Davison, took his children to the game as well and it was brilliant to share our love of the game with our youngsters.

The music of the 1960s was simply wonderful, with bands and artists as diverse as the Rolling Stones, the Beatles, Simon and Garfunkel and Gerry and the Pacemakers. I loved Frank Sinatra's song, Strangers in the Night, and, of course, My Way.

One Saturday night, we all got a lift in Johnny Anderson's car to the Top Hat Ballroom in Portstewart to hear Roy Orbison live, and he was amazing! What a great night. Unfortunately, Johnny had no patience to wait around and was always keen to get home quickly once the dance was over. Me and Packie Gillespie were too busy talking to some girls afterwards, because we were all trying to get Roy Orbison's autograph, and while we did, Johnny and the rest of the team headed off and left us stranded! As we didn't have money for a taxi, we started to thumb a lift back home to Derry – and we didn't even get Orbison's autograph!

As we were walking out the Coleraine Road in the hope that Johnny would come back to get us, a car stopped for us and gave us a lift to the bridge in Coleraine. I remember the driver was a Church of Ireland minister. After standing at the bridge for a few minutes, another car came along and stopped to give us a lift. It turned out the driver recognised us from the dance as they were the venue's bouncers who lived in Derry. We were very lucky, to be honest. Imagine if it had been during the far more dangerous 1970s and not in 1963 - we could have found ourselves in a very difficult situation.

Some of our friends went to England to find work as they had lost their jobs in Derry either in the 1960s or early 1970s. At that time, jobs were scarce and getting work in Derry could be extremely hard. I was lucky enough to have steady work from 1961 until 1979, but a lot of people were not so fortunate. Derry, Strabane, and Donegal suffered a great deal as a result of the partition of Ireland, and these areas had been totally neglected over many years by successive Irish, unionist, and British governments.

Throughout the 1960s, people in the North began to seriously question the dire housing conditions faced by many. Derry's housing problem was particularly atrocious, with families crammed into dilapidated, damp terraces, sometimes with different families living in every room in the house.

Thinking back to Bridge Street, I knew from first-hand experience just how bad the housing in Derry had become and we knew things had to change. High unemployment made matters worse, and the right to vote was denied to most Catholics. People began campaigning for change, and the civil rights movement pressured authorities for reform.

Sustained civil disobedience was successful in that it led to limited, long-overdue reforms. The Derry Corporation was disbanded, and voting rights were conceded. To address the housing situation and fairness of allocation, the Housing Executive was set up, removing the role of local councils.

When the Corporation was disbanded, the Derry Development Commission was set up, with its chairman Brian Morton and Vice Chairman, Stephen McGonagle. The Commission began a major new house-building programme in places on the outskirts of the city like Carnhill and Shantallow. This continued throughout the 1970s and led to the Greater Shantallow area as we know it today. The Derry Commission remained in place until the reform of local government in 1973.

I later got to know Stephen McGonagle very well during the 1980s as we both liked to swim at Templemore Sports Complex and would often have some great discussions in the sauna room afterwards. We'd talk about anything from politics to sport with others at the sauna, including Colum Holmes, Yachts McDermott, Charlie Bradley and others. I found Stephen to be a very learned and insightful person who could understand my politics but was himself a strong Labour man.

Stephen told me about a time when Terence O'Neill, then-Prime Minister of the North, had sent for him as he was the Ombudsman and they needed to discuss O'Neill's five-point reform programme to try and improve the situation for many across the North. O'Neill asked him when he should introduce these reforms, and Stephen told him emphatically, "Yesterday!" Stephen told us so many interesting stories and was so knowledgeable that I often said he should record his memoirs on tape. I hope he did.

There was a lot of talk about a civil rights march planned for 5 October 1968 in Derry, organised by the Northern Ireland Civil Rights Association (NICRA) and the Derry Housing Action Committee. The march had been banned under the Public Order Act, with Home Affairs minister William Craig claiming that the march was organised by republicans. While I knew something was badly wrong in our society, I only realised the full extent of our problems after the events of that day.

On the day of the march itself, Derry City were playing Distillery F.C. in the Brandywell grounds, and most of my friends and I went to the match. Afterwards, I was making my way back home towards Bridge Street when I heard from people that the RUC had attacked the Duke Street marchers, beating dozens indiscriminately. The whole town centre was filled with the RUC and their vehicles, as well as members of their auxiliary force, the dreaded B Specials.

That night was the first time I'd ever seen a riot and confrontation and petrol bombs. The RUC Victoria Barracks were attacked, and I thought to myself - this is the start of something that WILL change all our lives. We knew then that the civil rights movement was necessary as a means of overturning fifty years of unionist misrule. A few weeks later, Derry City were playing in the Brandywell again, but the football grounds were empty. Instead, we were all on the Craigavon Bridge and among a crowd of 20,000 singing We Shall Overcome. We knew that, from that moment on, we would all play different roles in what was to come.

Bray 1963, Lorny McIvor, Tony and John Hutton.

Tony, in tank-top, at the playpark on Abercorn Road in the 1950s with his father Gerry and younger brother Desmond.

Tony (right) with his father Gerry and brother Desmond outside their Bridge Street home in the 1950s.

A party, c1972, in John and Kay McFadden's house in Danesfort. Included are Michael and May Farren and Kay's mother. The McFaddens had put up the Hassans after the bomb destroyed their Bridge Street home.

A family trip to relatives in the country.

Tony's parents (on right) in Portstewart with best man Paddy Hassan.

With Lorny McIvor in the 1960s.

Tony, front, with his parents Gerry and Maggie, and brother Desmond.

A newspaper clipping reporting on the collapse of one of the gable houses at Bridge Street in the 1950s.

1. A fishing trip in Mayo. Included are Martin McGuinness, William McGuinness and James Quinn.
2. Tony would later admit that the violin lessons 'never quite took'.
3. Kevin Campbell, later Derry Mayor, and Damien Doherty (d) at a Volunteers Dinner.

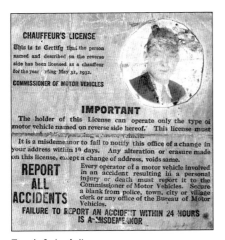

Tony's father's licence.

Tony's mother Margaret (née McGuire) on her bike, at the Buncrana Cinema, alongside friends Maisie McLaughlin, Suzie McLoone and Mary Redden.

Tony's younger sister, Ann Fox

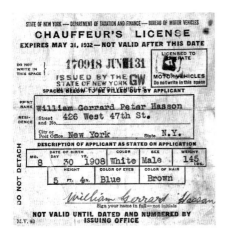

Gerry Hasson's Chauffeur's License.

Tony's father, Gerry (glasses) at work as a winch-driver on the docks.

43

1. Tony, Chrissie and granddaughter Tara.
2. Front right, at a meeting in the TGWU Hall, Orchard Street to discuss the closure of the BSR plant in Creggan, where Tony worked in the 1960s.
3. Tony with grandchildren Tara and Oisín at an Easter rally.

Lorny McIvor bears the weight of Packie McIvor for this photo outside their chalet.

Tony and his sister, Ann Fox at an event in Pitcher's, 2017.

Fifth from right, with glasses, is Tony's father, Gerry Hassan, who was a winch-operator at the docks. Tony himself often worked Saturday mornings at the docks, after his week's work at the BSR and could earn more there than at his regular job. In the 1950s, a 'Scotch Boat' from Glasgow would dock every second day, later reducing that service to once a week, before eventually stopping.

John Gibbons, Tony and John Hutton in Bray in the 1960s.

An early picture of Tony and Chrissie (right) in Butlins, where they met in the 1960s. Also included are Lorny McIvor, and Barney Kelly - who was later killed in the Top of the Hill Massacre.

Tony's family and friends at a presentation dinner in his honour. Included are his son Ciarán, wife Chrissie and daughter Áine.

Tony with Peter 'Duck' McDonald at an Easter march.

With Lorny McIvor in Bray, 1963.

47

Derry men on holidays: Packie Gillespie and Lorny McIvor, with two friends at Butlins.

Tony and Lecky Road man John Millar outside their Butlins chalet. John would later die from cancer at a tragically-young age.

The Hassan family at the old City Hotel, 1960.

1. Tony and friends in Bray in the 1960s
2. Tony, now driving, in Dublin with friends for a Gaelic match in 1966.
3. Tony's mother Margaret (Maggie) welcomes Gerry Bradley to a New Year's Eve celebration at the Hassan home.
4. Derry men on Dublin's Ha'penny Bridge. Included are Tony, John Millar, Lorny McIvor and Bernard McMonagle.

1. A gather up football match at the BSR (Birmingham Sound Reproducers) factory in Creggan during lunch break. Included are Joe Doherty, Tony Coyle, John Millar and Tony.
2. The young cowboy.
3. Getting some sun, Lorny McIvor, John Millar and Tony.

At Bradley's Pass, overseeing the final touches being made to the development at the junction of Racecourse Drive.

Dockers at Derry Quay in the 1950s.

1. The BSR factory on Bligh's Lane where Tony worked in the 1960s.
2. The top of Bridge Street, home (among others) to Jim Clifford, later an SDLP councillor in Creggan.

An attempted British army jeep outside the Shantallow shops in the late 1970s. Republicans had a siren installed at the Sinn Féin caravan beside the shops, which they would sound when they wanted locals to assemble.

The Castle outside Buncrana, where Tony's parents would take them on holiday in the 1950s.

The former GNR railway station on Foyle Street.

Development at lower Skeoge, close to Pine Trees.

1. The Casbah Bar at the top of Orchard Street, close to Tony's family home. The pub was later immortalised in the Undertones' song Casbah Rock.
2. Bridge Street
3. Shantallow shops bearing the graffiti, 'Join the army and murder'.
4. Bridge Street in the 1970s, at the start of the redevelopment of the area

1. Bridge Street pictured in the 1970s before redevelopment. In the foreground is the crater left after the collapse of McIntyre's Bar
2. Buncrana Castle, where the Hassan family would holiday in the 1950s.

The old Bridge Street School, shortly before its demolition.

Orchard Street shortly before the development of Foyleside in the 1990s.

The Hayloft Bar at the bottom of Bridge Street in the 1970s. The Sailor's Rest building on the corner with Foyle Road, which was run by the Methodists, was formerly a hotel and mini-cinema. The British army also occupied the building in the early Troubles.

Tony, pictured here at the Damien House complex on Foyle Road, has been a lifelong campaigner to eliminate homelessness.

Photographs of deceased Shantallow Volunteers on display at the Monument.

The new Health & Wellbeing Centre at Leafair.

CHAPTER 6
The Battle of the Bogside

Everything changed for us then as the civil rights movement gained momentum and took over all our lives. We went to meetings, we marched and protested, and did what we could. It felt like the swinging sixties were now over, and a new era had begun.

From October to the end of that year, we demonstrated when we could. The constant hostility from both the RUC and the B Specials spurred us further and made us even more determined to keep on protesting. Baton charges and blocking demonstrations would never stop us. We wanted an end to the widespread discrimination and inadequate housing. We wanted more jobs and one man, one vote. We were determined.

On New Year's Day 1969, a civil rights march had been organised by the Belfast-led People's Democracy marching from Belfast to Derry over four days. As the peaceful marchers neared their destination on January 4, they were ambushed by loyalist gangs, off-duty RUC men and B Specials at Burntollet Bridge, a few miles outside the city. Many marchers were injured.

I was in Guildhall Square waiting for them to come in after their four-day journey to get here. The whole of Foyle Street was lined with people down to the Melville Hotel and beyond. As the march made its way into Derry's centre, it was attacked again by loyalists in the city's Waterside before getting a sensational welcome from the thousands of people lining the whole of Foyle Street and Guildhall Square. We waited for the marchers to come back. We listened to some speeches, and we could clearly see by looking at the marchers around us that something had happened on the way to Derry because they were battered, bloodied and exhausted. A lot of them had been hit by RUC batons and stones and they bled openly from head wounds while they stood there in Guildhall Square. It transpired later that they had been ambushed by the RUC and armed loyalists along the route from Burntollet into the city.

We all headed back over William Street and intense rioting broke out for a couple of hours.

Earlier that day, the RUC and B Specials had entered the Bogside and caused widespread damage to homes in the area. Their incursion caused community activists and residents to react by building barricades to prevent the RUC from entering the area again. You were always dubious about the B Specials and police. The RUC were well known as a sectarian and a Protestant police force, and the community had enough. That early morning after Burntollet, the B-Men invaded the Bogside and caused chaos in The Wells, smashing a lot of windows and kicking-in the front doors of the pensioners who lived there.

Tensions remained high over the next few weeks and months. By the summer of 1969, the six counties were like a powder keg ready to explode. The actions of the RUC and their violent baton attacks against nationalists was repeated throughout the six counties.

Although I did hang around in the Bogside, I lived in Bridge Street and so I was often stopped or noticed walking home every night. The B-Specials in particular tended to stop me going up Fahan Street.

Even in the showband days before that and before the civil rights movement started, we were hassled coming home from dances or getting off the bus from the Plaza and Borderlands dance halls. Sometimes you weren't stopped, but if you were, it was either at Butcher Gate or Ferryquay Gate. The RUC/B-men would ask where you were coming from and where you were going, generally throwing their weight around. This was long before civil rights. They were always as intimidating.

The events that transpired over those few weeks in July and August 1969 were to change people's attitudes further, with more and more people getting involved with the civil right movement and protests swelled in numbers.

As usual, these peaceful demos were met by force as the RUC continued to fulfil the role given to them since the establishment of the Orange State in 1922 – keeping nationalists firmly in their place. But the civil rights movement now had the support of a younger generation who were not prepared to go back to what our elders had endured for so long.

One of the first people to die at the hands of the RUC was 67-year-old Francis McCloskey from Dungiven on 13 July 1969. The first fatality of the Troubles, Francis was standing in the doorway of Hassan's Drapery – no relation to us – when police baton-charged a crowd and he was hit on the head with a police baton causing a brain haemorrhage. He died the next day in hospital.

Sammy Devenny was beaten by the RUC on 19 April 1969, which was a Saturday. There had been a march organised for that day, but we got word back to Guildhall Square that the march had been cancelled. We were about to disperse except for the fact that there were loyalists and Paisleyites within the Guildhall, you see, and they took no notice of any cancellations. A loyalist crowd started throwing stones at us. The RUC responded to this provocation by attacking us too, and all hell broke loose. It ended in fierce rioting and the RUC sealing off the Bogside.

My foremost memory of that time is that they the Paisleyites came out and saw the crowd gathered around Guildhall Square and they used whatever they had at hand for weapons, as usual, breaking off the legs of chairs and tables to fight with The RUC, instead of getting into the Paisleyites, they beat us back over to William Street, as was always the way. Every civil rights event, the RUC was on the side of the loyalists

During the rioting that night, the RUC followed fleeing rioters as they ran through the open door of the Devenny home in William Street to escape the police. At that time during riots, if the cops were running after people they tended to run for their lives and if they ran in through your door, that was expected. Father-of-nine Sammy had been standing in his doorway talking to neighbours when RUC officers smashed their way into the house and began beating everyone in sight. They beat Sammy almost to death as well as attacking several of his young children and the two visiting neighbours, Freddie Budd and Paddy Harkin. Sammy was severely beaten on the head and body and hospitalised for a long time afterwards. The town went crazy after that. There was an anger there, but you weren't scared. Dubious at times certainly.

Shortly after Sammy got out of hospital, he suffered a fatal heart attack in his home on 17 July 1969. His death was blamed on the RUC, and his funeral was one of the biggest crowds the city had ever seen. The death of Sammy Devenny was the final straw for Bogsiders, and Free Derry was born.

In 1969, Bernadette Devlin was an agreed candidate and elected MP For Mid-Ulster in the British parliament. Bernadette used her position as MP to try and make the British government understand the Irish question and the fundamental change needed.

Historically, the North's unionist government and the Protestant Orange Order had used their position and annual Twelfth parades to remind nationalists of their second-class citizenship. Members of the Orange Order were called Orangemen, including the Apprentice Boys of Derry who annually held contentious marches through Derry to commemorate the 1689 Siege of Derry.

In 1969, things became even more sinister as unionists reacted angrily to the growing civil rights movement, again accusing it of being a republican takeover. This only added to loyalism's anger and made loyalists even more determined to attack the peaceful movement - fully aware that they had the support and endorsement of the both the RUC and B Specials.

Looking back at just how bitter loyalists could be against the nationalist people, I tend to think that they were used by the unionist government and its sectarian police force. After all, loyalist communities across the North were no better off than we were, with equally as dismal a housing situation. Yet I feel they were encouraged and expected to take sides and attack the civil rights movement that was trying to bring about meaningful change.

The actions of the RUC had become so notorious by summer 1969, many were apprehensive of the forthcoming Apprentice Boys' Twelfth parades through Catholic areas of the city. The parade was a minefield and likely to spark widespread trouble, and professional people throughout the city, including the clergy, urged organisers to reroute the orange march away from the Bogside.

As usual, the unionists did not listen to the community's concerns and so all hell broke loose. Rioting broke out across the area as members of the Bogside battled to keep RUC and loyalist rioters out of their area. The Battle of the Bogside had started.

It was by now clear that the North was on fire. I was on holidays when Battle of the Bogside kicked off, and we waited patiently as news filtered through from Derry about what was happening. Locally, the Derry Citizens Defence Association was set up by Sean Keenan, Paddy Doherty, Johnnie White and others. The group quickly set about sealing off all the entrances and exits to the Bogside and Creggan in a bid to keep their neighbourhoods safe.

First-aid posts were established at various points, and a radio transmitter heralded the beginning of Radio Free Derry - a community-led initiative that broadcast messages calling for resistance and for people to come help defend the Bogside. It also broadcast regular news bulletins from Barricade Joe, providing the community with updates during this battle with the RUC and its loyalist supporters. For the first time, the RUC fired CS gas into the Bogside to incapacitate locals, and CS gas continued to be fired across the days of fighting.

On 13 August – the second day of the stand-off – Irish Taoiseach Jack Lynch delivered a televised appeal for calm and promising help in the form of field hospitals just over the border - but this help never came. People who were injured were still taken to hospitals across the border, as to seek medical help at Derry's Altnagelvin Hospital would have risked arrest and incarceration. I remember Jack Lynch did march the Irish troops up to the border and then marched them back again. We knew then that there would be no support from Dublin. The turmoil enveloping Derry soon spread to Belfast as word of events filtered out.

By the third day of the stand-off, it was clear to authorities that the RUC had been defeated in the Bogside. Then came the announcement that British soldiers were to be deployed to the North.

Meanwhile, whole streets in Catholic areas of Belfast were attacked and set alight by loyalist mobs over the same few days. Bombay Street was burned out by loyalists throwing incendiaries into homes in the West Belfast estate. In another area, a nine-year-old boy called Patrick Rooney was shot and killed through the walls of his own Divis Flats' home when patrolling RUC officers opened fire with a heavy-calibre machine gun, spraying residential buildings on the estate. The events across Belfast claimed a total of eight lives.

The British army first appeared in the North on 14 August, arriving at the edge of the Bogside at around teatime as the RUC were withdrawn from the area. The Derry Citizens Defence Association declared their intention to continue defending the area against both the RUC and the British army until their demands were met.

As a gesture of goodwill, local representatives agreed to remove the barricades at the Bogside and replace them with a symbolic white line that the British army wouldn't cross. The army made no attempt to enter the area.

Back then, we thought Bernadette Devlin and Eamonn McCann were the people to follow. I always respected McCann because he was steadfast in what he was doing.

I remember seeing Bernadette Devlin on the barricade about three days after the Brits came in and took up their positions around the city. She told people off for giving tea and sandwiches to the British army. I remember that she always gave them their full title, the British army and not the Brits. She said something like "Cast your mind back to when they came in here last Thursday - which direction were they facing? They were facing into the Bogside, not facing our enemies." It came to pass after the Honeymoon period with the Brits was over, that Bernadette was exactly right.

We arrived back in Derry to desperate scenes. The British army stopped us going over the border, and that was the first time we'd ever seen them. At the Craigavon Bridge, another massive queue of cars were waiting as the Brits checked all the traffic going into the city.

After the Battle of the Bogside, the Derry Defence Association organised a Fleadh Cheoil to celebrate the effort that the community had put into the battle. The Dubliners, the Clancy Brothers and other groups performed outside the Bogside Inn for most of the night, and the atmosphere was tremendous. I remember it well and we all had a great time.

Initial good relations between the British army and the nationalist community grew worse as the weeks and months passed. It was becoming clear that what Bernadette Devlin said was coming to pass - the Brits were merely here to prop up and protect British and unionist interests in Ireland.

CHAPTER 7
Settling Down

I met my wife Christine in 1966 while on holiday at Butlin's Holiday Camp. We kept in touch afterwards, and because I had a car it was easy to drive down to Dublin to see her some weekends, and Christine would come up to Derry on others.

It wasn't the best of times to travel as border checks were getting particularly harsh. Coming up from Dublin in the middle of a war-zone must have been difficult for Christine as our romance progressed, but we saw each other when we could – most weekends, holiday times and at Christmas-time. Christine's family always made me so welcome, and we spent time with her sister Lily, her brother-in-law Frank, and her niece Claire. At times when I was there for the weekend, we'd go for a drink with another sister, Rita, and her husband Jerry Dempsey.

Christine and I got married on March 31, 1970 in Ballyfermot Chapel, Dublin, and our wedding reception was held that evening in the Royal Hotel in Dun Laoghaire. Most of the mates I'd spent the 1960s with were at the wedding, including John Hutton, Packie, Micky McIvor, and John Gibbons. My brother Dessie was my Best Man.

For our honeymoon, we toured Ireland in a new Ford Escort which I had hired out for two weeks. Then came the harder part of looking for somewhere to live. We searched all over the city, but housing was still ridiculous with the cost of renting even a one-room flat beyond the average budget.

My mother invited us to stay with them in the family home in Bridge Street while we saved for a house. She also advised us to join a building society and to aim for a house down in Danesfort Crescent in the Shantallow area on the outskirts of the city. At that time, a new house in Danesfort was £4,000 or £5,000 and not taking her advice was one of the biggest mistakes we made.

We stayed in Bridge Street until September 1971 when disaster struck our homes on a quiet Saturday evening. Christine and my mother were hanging out the washing in the backyard when my mother smelled smoke – she had a great sense of smell. They opened the gate to the back lane and saw a box there with smoke billowing out.

Right away, my ma and Christine raised the alarm and got everyone out of the house. Everyone except my father, who refused to move because he was watching horse-racing on TV and had money on Lester Piggott for the treble. He shouted at her, "Maggie, hold on till the race is over! Piggott is leading!" We did get him out of the house though, and then realised that my brother Dessie was still in bed in the house after the night shift in DuPont.

I ran back into the house and was halfway up the stairs when the bomb went off. All I saw was daylight as the entire back section of our home fell into the back lane. We were lucky no-one was killed, but young Georgie White was injured by a section of roof that blew off the houses and hit him. The whole place was a bomb site, with as many as thirty houses in our part of the street wrecked or damaged by the blast.

It was pandemonium afterwards, with people wandering in a daze and crying. I remember seeing Rose, who owned the American Bar, coming up the street with a bottle of brandy and giving us all a stiff drink. The RUC and British army were on the scene quickly enough, as were local priests and people from the Housing Executive trying to assess the situation. Later that day, my father heard that Lester Piggott had won the race and he'd got his treble up.

These houses in Bridge Street were not liveable after the blast, and so some people went to stay with relatives or friends. Because it was the weekend, there was little that could be done until Monday anyway.

Chrissie and I needed a place to stay, too, and were advised to try again with the Housing Executive. Although we went to the Shantallow Community Centre where Fr Mulvey had organised help for people caught up in the bomb, we still didn't get a flat at that time.

The Housing Executive did deliver for most of the Bridge Street families, however. My mother got a letter from them on the Monday evening after the bomb and they were allocated a new house at 397 Carnhill. The next day I took my mother down to her new home in Carnhill and I recall it was a lovely, sunny summer's day. You could smell the fresh paint from the new houses.

She looked around, then went upstairs to have a look. When she came back down, she was crying. When I asked her, "Mother, why are you crying?" I remember she said tearfully she never thought she would have a house with an inside toilet and bathroom. I'm sure many people felt the same seeing their brand new homes after the bleak, overcrowded housing conditions people had endured for so many years.

I should explain why I think the bomb was placed in our back lane in Bridge Street. Back then, the British army had moved into the building at the back of our homes that had previously been a hotel owned by the Kelly family, and then became the Sailor's Rest. Since then, it had been lying derelict for some time so when the army arrived in 1969, they took over the building for two years. But the bomb had actually caused more damage to our homes than to its intended army target.

It was a reckless thing to do, in my opinion. If a bomb warning was given, then nobody in our street had received it. I often wonder what would have happened if my mother and Christine hadn't been out hanging the washing that day and smelled something. No doubt our lives would have been changed forever.

The family soon moved into their new home and loved it there. They still had some neighbours from Bridge Street nearby as others had also got homes in the new Carnhill estate. A few weeks after that, my wife and I finally got a one-bedroom flat.

The Bishop of Derry, Bishop Farren, gave £100 to every family whose home was damaged by the bomb to help them get started in their new homes. This gesture was much appreciated by the families.

Christine and I had two children, our son Ciarán was born on 21 January 1974, and our daughter Áine on 16 July 1977. After Ciarán was born, we began looking for a three-bedroom house as the one-bedroom flat was, by now, too small. But the Housing Executive wouldn't allocate us a house because I was on rent and rates strike. The strike had been organised by the Civil Rights Association as a form of civil disobedience. We had been told during a huge public meeting in the Brandywell football stadium that we shouldn't pay the money back but should spend it.

These same people later got elected and formed the first Assembly in the North. The first thing they did once elected was to impose a collection charge on the same people that they'd instructed not to pay rent, and this subsequently allowed the Housing Executive to refuse those with outstanding house arrears a new house. On principle, I wouldn't pay the money I owed to the Housing Executive, but as time went on and Ciarán was almost four years old, I knew I had to give in and pay. Again, my mother came to the rescue giving me the £75 needed to pay off the Housing Executive, which was a lot of money to pay up-front in those days.

After that, we were finally allocated a house at 46 Moss Park by Paddy McIntyre, the then manager of the Housing Executive in Shantallow. We moved into our new house and the following year, Áine was born.

My siblings also settled down and got married. My sister, Ann, married Michael Fox and together they had three children, Caoimhe, Gearoid and

Mairead. For a while they also lived in Carnhill, but they later moved to Belfield Park in Foyle Springs.

Ann had worked in Molins factory at Maydown until it closed. After that, she worked at several other places including at Derry City Football Club as Jim McLaughlin's secretary. She dealt with match tickets, the Derry City Draw and the player's wages, and also later worked under Noel King and Roy Coyle.

I was disappointed when the Derry City story was recently covered in a TV documentary that Ann didn't get a mention. Having had such a long association with the club, I do feel she should have got a mention.

After leaving Derry City, Ann became involved with Weight Watchers and worked there until she took ill some years later. She developed a brain tumour and got extremely sick, and this was a huge tragedy for the family as Ann was always the backbone of our family. If we had any problems, Ann was always there to help and, in most cases, sort things out. Ann had the same streak of kindness as Aunt Agnes, always giving and never taking. Towards the end, Ann spent eighteen weeks in the Foyle Hospice and died on December 4, 2017. We were devastated and still think of Ann every day. I doubt we'll ever get over her death.

With two brothers growing up, my sister Ann always wanted a sister and so when I met Christine, they took to each other straight away. Not only were they the best of friends, but they were also close as any real sisters could be. When Ann died, it broke Christine's heart just as much as it did ours. Ann's husband, Michael, died four years after she did on 22 February 2022.

My brother Dessie married Hilda Cunningham and they had four children, Nicola, Leona, Conarie and Donal in Daisyhill Park before moving to Culmore. When Conarie was about nine, he was knocked down by a car at the junction of Steelstown Road and Madam's Bank Road and left in a coma for almost three months.

Naturally, the whole family feared the worst but our Ann, as always, was a pillar of strength and positivity insisting he would pull through. She was right, of course. He took a long time to recover, but the important thing is that he did, and he went on to marry a girl called Caroline and they have a good life together.

Christine's sister in Dublin, Rita, and her brother-in-law Jerry had six of a family, Alan, Paul, Derek, Darren, Karl and a daughter called Gillian. When my own children were young, they loved to spend a few weeks of their summer holidays with their relatives in Dublin. Áine always said that the trip to Dublin began with a packet crisps and drink from the Bus Station shop and a stop at Monaghan for a snack.

Ciarán loved staying in Rita's with her boys as they had a caravan at the holiday resort in Rush and always had a mad time there. Darren and Ciarán were thick as thieves, too, always in trouble or causing mischief together. Derek was the singer of Rita's house and still is today. He's living in America and still entertaining people in New York nightclubs.

Áine and Chrissie often stayed with Chrissie's other sister Lily, too, and according to Áine, Auntie Lily made the most amazing eggs and chips! Both of my children loved being able to spend those early holidays in Dublin.

Áine and Ciarán have all grown up now and have had families of their own, making Chrissie and myself grandparents. Ciarán married Maureen and together, they had five children, Dearbhaile, Callum, Niamh, Conall and Caoimhín.

Áine has two children of her own, Tara and Oisín, so we're very lucky.

CHAPTER 8
Civil Rights and Internment

After the RUC and B Specials were beaten back and lost control at the Battle of the Bogside, things were relatively quiet for a while. It was common to see the Brits chatting with locals, and people would sometimes bring the soldiers out cups of tea and baps too.

I was still mindful of what Bernadette Devlin had said after the Brits' arrival in 1969, and this sense of unease grew. Gradually, the army began stopping and questioning people, and being harassed at army checkpoints became a daily occurrence. Then things escalated with army house raids and families would have their doors kicked in and homes damaged. There were also riots whenever these house raids took place.

The civil rights movement continued nonetheless, with meetings, marches and protests organised when the need arose. Deliberately non-violent, these protests were still met with the same RUC heavy-handedness as before.

I was one of about 500 protesters who engaged in a sit-down protest at the junction of Laburnum Terrace and Westland Street. The Brits, through a loudspeaker, told us to disperse but of course we didn't move. It seemed to me that most marches had John Hume and Ivan Cooper at the front. Cooper urged us not to move, but the Brits had a water cannon that squirted purple dye at crowds and if you were identified by this dye, you could be arrested.

People started to run and so did I, until I looked around and saw Harry Mallett shouting at us to get back. As I turned back, I was hit with the water cannon dye right on the face! Hume, Cooper, and Hugh Logue were all arrested that day, and someone took a photo of them standing, soaked and spread-eagled, against the wall of Alex Orr's shop in Laburnum Terrace. I ducked quickly into someone's house and managed to clean most of the incriminating dye off my face before going back out to the protest.

The situation in the North grew worse as the months passed, and throughout 1970 and 1971 the Brits continually harassed and intimidated nationalist people all over the six counties. The house raids and checkpoints escalated, as did the army's hostility to us in general.

After a republican conference in Dublin in December 1969, the IRA divided into separate 'Official' and 'Provisional' movements. The Provisional IRA (the

Provos) were adamant that areas in the North had to be defended at all costs.

Unlike during the Battle of the Bogside, Derry was now defended by well-armed members of the IRA, and republicans started to build the movement in the city. Volunteers were mostly from the area or environs, and the organisation launched regular attacks against the British army. Within the communities themselves, support for the IRA swelled as more and more nationalists were targeted, injured or shot dead by the Brits with no justification.

*

Tragedy struck on June 27, 1970 when a premature explosion went off in a family home in Dunree Gardens in Creggan. It killed Thomas McCool and his two young daughters - eight year-old Bernadette, and her three year-old sister, Carole. Joe Coyle was also killed, and another man, Tommy Carlin, died two weeks later. They had been making a bomb in the kitchen when it went off, killing the sleeping children upstairs. Another daughter survived because she was asleep on the sofa downstairs. News of the two girls' deaths devastated all of Derry – such an unbelievable catastrophe for the McCool family.

McCool and Carlin were seen as the leaders of the Republican Movement in the city so there was great sadness at their loss within the movement too.

Things only got worse. On the morning of July 8, 1971, a young, unarmed Derry man called Seamus Cusack was shot by the Brits and died on the way to hospital. Later that day as people reacted to Cusack's death, the army shot dead another man, teenager Dessie Beattie. He was only nineteen and unarmed. They tried to say later he was throwing nail-bombs.

On August 18, 1971, the Brits tried to break through no-go areas of Derry, drafting in helicopters and well over a thousand soldiers but the barricades stood strong. IRA Volunteer Eamon Lafferty was shot dead by the army during a gun-battle in Creggan, aged 19 years-old. Also in August, another Volunteer, Jim O'Hagan, was killed in a shooting accident. A 14 year-old schoolgirl, Annette McGavigan, was shot dead by Brits stationed on the Derry Walls on September 6, then Billy McGreanery, another innocent civilian, was shot dead on September 15. He was killed at Laburnum Terrace by a British soldier of the Grenadier Guards.

Communities protested loudly against the army's murderous actions and openly opposed the Brits in whatever way they could. There were riots every other day as people engaged in running battles with the army, and the army baton-charged rioters, more barricades were set up, and the sight of petrol bombs became commonplace.

There were also gun battles between the IRA and the Brits, and British soldiers were killed in exchanges with the IRA. This was war, and to date, none of the deaths caused by the police or army half a century ago have received genuine truth or justice.

The unionist government couldn't contain the North of 1969, and once again, they increasingly lost control of the situation in the early 1970s. When new Stormont prime minister, Brian Faulkner, took over in March 1971, tensions continued to escalate. To stamp out republican and nationalist unrest, Faulkner and the British government then announced internment without trial so the army could lift and detain people indefinitely.

When they launched internment on August 9, over 300 men were lifted and interned, causing widespread riots everywhere. Faulkner thought that his actions would sort out the problem that existed in the North, but it was obvious that the unionist regime could no longer control Northern Ireland. The very existence of the state was being challenged by the people in Derry and the IRA, whose ranks were swollen with new recruits responding to internment. I feel that the republican message reflected a feeling shared by many in the Catholic community, that the only way to reform the state was to smash it.

The army rounded people up from every part of the North, and before long the identities of some of those arrested became known to us. There were quite a few people that I knew in Shantallow were taken aboard the prison ship Maidstone in Belfast Lough. Seventeen year-old Martin Bones O'Neill, 18 year-old Martin Cookie Lynch and Frankie Lindsay were all interned on that ship.

Throughout the decades, both unionist and British politicians have blamed the IRA for starting the conflict, but in my opinion, they brought it on themselves through their history of misrule and mistreatment of the nationalist people of the Six Counties. The British government supported and aided this oppression as it happened. Battling against the civil rights movement and alienating nationalist people had galvanised those very communities and others. They forced people's backs against the wall, but our generation wasn't going to lie down and take it - and they came out fighting.

The civil rights movement was still active, with peaceful protests against interment every week and other civil disobedience when we could. Meanwhile, there was growing activity from the IRA too.

I visited Long Kesh, the prison that became the Maze, a few times to see Pat And his Brother Kieran McColgan and Robbie Davison who were detained there. I also went to see our Cumann chairperson, Jim Breslin, who was interned too, and to the Crumlin Road and Armagh prisons to see friends and comrades. Those were dark days, and Long Kesh was the worst of all - intimidating from the minute people arrived at its gate.

CHAPTER 9
BLOODY SUNDAY

The fury of youths armed with stones and petrol-bombs grew fiercer as anger at the British army and authorities spilled over. Adding to the community's frustrations were reports emerging from detention centres of widespread mistreatment and torture by British interrogators. It was soon apparent that the interrogation methods they used were not merely rough-handling by undisciplined soldiers, but well-rehearsed brutal techniques used by trained specialists. When we heard about the Hooded Men and what they were put through at torture centres, we were all furious.

In November 1971, the Southern government passed the allegations of brutality to the European Court of Human Rights demonstrating that, on this occasion, Dublin wasn't prepared to publicly identify itself with internment. The British government were questioned but not sanctioned over the many reports of internment, torture and shootings. The British army had also been involved in a massacre in Ballymurphy over the few August days when they launched internment. Eleven civilians lost their lives in Ballymurphy, and the soldiers behind it were the Parachute Regiment. This was six months before they were sent in on Bloody Sunday.

At the beginning of November 1971, the British army shot dead a Derry mother called Kathleen Thompson in the garden of her home in the Creggan estate. Her murder left six children without a mother, and those same children then had to wait almost fifty years for an inquest into her death. Justice is denied to Kathleen's daughter, Minty, and her siblings.

Four people were killed by rubber and plastic bullets fired by police and army in Derry over the years. Harry Duffy, Stephen McConomy and Paul Whitters were killed with plastic bullets, and Thomas Friel by rubber bullet. Altogether, there were seventeen people killed across the North, eight of whom were children. Let's not forget Richard Moore, who was blinded by a rubber bullet when he was a child in Derry, and many more who were injured over the years.

By the beginning of 1972, many areas across the North felt like war zones. In Derry, the civil rights association were busy organising an anti-internment march through the city on January 30, calling on the British government to end all practices of internment. After what happened in Ballymurphy, we were overly concerned about what might happen to us if we protested, and some called for the march to be cancelled.

Leading up to the march, word spread that it would be stopped by the Brits and again, we thought of what the army did in Ballymurphy. On the week of the march itself, we noticed more and more British army personnel coming into the city, heavily armed. Two days before came the rumour that the British Paratroop Regiment were being considered for Derry and that did not look good.

That Sunday morning was just like any normal Sunday with people coming in from chapel and waiting for dinner. Afterwards, we made our way to the Bishop's Field in Creggan, and the 20,000 or so people there were all in good spirits. It was a carnival-like event. The Civil Rights Association's plan was to march from Creggan to the Guildhall Square via William Street, but the British army was prepared and blocked the parade from making its way to the Guildhall Square. The route through William Street had been closed off with barbed wire and armoured vehicles, and march organisers rerouted the rally away from William Street and into the Bogside to Free Derry Corner.

Most of the march turned into Rossville Street, but some of the youths broke away and ran towards the army barricades at William Street. They hurled abuse and stones at the British troops, and, in turn, the troops fired back with rubber bullets, tear gas and a water cannon.

Skirmishes between youths and the army were not uncommon at that time, so nobody was surprised when they heard that stone-throwing and rioting had kicked off at the army's barrier.

The majority of the rally ignored the clashes at William Street and moved towards Free Derry Corner where there were speakers lined up to address the people.

John Hutton and I went with the march towards Free Derry Corner and as we got there, we heard people getting more and more anxious worrying about what might happen. Then came news that paratroopers had been seen near the Guildhall, and within a matter of minutes, the British Parachute Regiment drove into the Bogside. Its soldiers jumped from their armoured vehicles and opened fire into the fleeing crowds. They gunned down unarmed civilians, most of whom had their back to the soldiers as they tried to get away. With all this going on, I hit the ground and stayed low. I could see the platform with the speakers now jumping off it to find cover, and it was the first time I felt really, really scared.

I saw people helping Lord Brockway off the platform. I also saw chippings flying off the top of Free Derry Corner as bullets hit it from the direction of the Derry Walls. That distinct feeling that they were shooting from the walls was what made me stay close to the ground, although it was never proven at the Bloody Sunday Inquiry. In my mind, it had to come from the walls. I was lying on the ground and when I looked up, I saw bits coming off the wall in such a way that it seemed clear they were shooting towards us from the Derry Walls.

As shooting continued all around us, I was lying on the ground and couldn't move for fear. Looking around me, I could see that everybody else was doing the same, just trying to stay out of the line of army fire.

It must have been about fifteen minutes or so before we started to move again and get up from our crouched positions. I couldn't see my friend John anymore, but I met one of the Flood family - a friend of my sister Ann - and she took me to her house where I stayed for a few hours. The street outside was in a terrible panic, and we could still hear people shouting and screaming and running away from the gunfire.

A few people came into the house while I was there to tell us there were three people shot dead – then it was five people, then eight people. It was so scary it's difficult to explain just how we felt. It was a nightmare. I remember thinking, "Sweet Jesus, there's eight dead now." We were all thinking to ourselves, Holy fuck - this is crazy.

After an hour or more, someone came to the house to tell us that twenty people had been shot or injured, and many of those were dead. We just couldn't believe it. As the numbers of the injured and dead kept rising, we got more and more scared. There was no word of thirteen dead yet. I didn't hear that until later when we got back to our house that night. Chrissie was worrying because she didn't know where I was, so she was relieved to find out I was okay.

It was dark when I finally got out of that house in Meenan Park and there was a deadness in the Bogside. It's a feeling and an experience that will never leave me.

Father Edward Daly, a highly respected priest who went to become the Bishop of Derry, was witness to the army's behaviour on Bloody Sunday and he publicly condemned the paratroopers afterwards for firing indiscriminately into crowds.

He told a TV reporter afterwards, "It was utterly disgraceful. They were firing lead bullets in all directions, there was nothing fired at them, I can say that with absolute certainty because I was there. The people were running in all directions. Most of them had their backs turned to them and they just opened fire."

Father Daly was there when the paratroopers first entered the Bogside, and he ran from their vehicles alongside a boy called Jackie Duddy. Jackie was shot in the back and died on the street. Daly and others had tried to help him, but it was too late. It was the same for so many others that day. Of course, the Brits were quick to claim that everyone they shot were either gunmen or nail bombers – a lie they would stick to for decades.

Derry was like a graveyard for days afterwards. People couldn't quite take in what had just happened in our city, it seemed so unbelievable. I remember there was an overwhelming feeling of silence and stillness in the air for so long afterwards. A sense of shock and disbelief quickly spread around Ireland and caused widespread protests. Riots in the Republic of Ireland culminated in the burning-down of its British Embassy in Dublin.

The British government had just made the biggest mistake in their history. In thinking Bloody Sunday would sort the Irish problem, it had the opposite effect. The army's actions on Bloody Sunday, and their cover-up afterwards, gave the Republican Movement and IRA its biggest recruitment surge ever.

The British Paratroop Regiment shot dead thirteen men and boys on January 30 1972, and most were running away. Eighteen other people were injured, including a mother of 14 children who was shot and left with terrible injuries, and a teenage girl crushed by an army Saracen. All those who died or were wounded are listed here.

Jackie Duddy (17)
Hugh Gilmour (17)
Michael Kelly (17)
Michael McDaid (20)
John Young (17)
William Nash (19)
Kevin McElhinney (17)
William McKinney (27)
Jim Wray (22)
Gerald Donaghey (17)
Gerard McKinney (35)
Patrick Doherty (31)
Bernard McGuigan (41)
John Johnston (59, died 16 June 1972)

Wounded:
Damian Donaghy (15)
Alana Burke (18)
Thomas Harkin (18))
Peggy Deery (31)
Patsy McDaid (25)
Pius McCarron (30)
Patrick Brolly (40)
Mickey Bridge (25)
Michael Bradley (22)
Alexander Nash (51)
Patsy O'Donnell (41)
Joseph Mahon (16)
Michael Quinn (17)
Joseph Friel (20)
Danny Gillespie (32)
Patrick Campbell (51)
Daniel McGowan (38)

John Johnson raised the total number of dead to fourteen when he died of his injuries a few months later on 16 June 1972. prematurely as a result of his injuries and the trauma he suffered that day.

It is now fifty years since Bloody Sunday, and as I'm writing this book the families of those killed and wounded are still without justice from the British.

CHAPTER 10
Taking Sides

Things changed after Bloody Sunday. Derry felt like a ghost town for a long time afterwards as we struggled to accept the army's actions, and what that meant in terms of our supposedly peaceful civil rights movement. This new reality was hard to believe and anger and frustration swelled.

In the days and weeks after Bloody Sunday, the IRA could hardly cope with the sheer numbers wanting to join up and had to turn people away. It's clear in hindsight that Bloody Sunday was probably the single biggest recruitment drive the IRA ever had. The army thought they were teaching us a lesson and putting us in our place, but it had completely the opposite effect.

I suppose a lot of us felt we had to choose a side because the idea of a non-violent civil rights movement now felt destroyed - the British had seen to that. I took the republican side as I saw no hope for a peaceful way forward after the things I witnessed on Bloody Sunday. It was impossible. It changed my life, and the lives of every person on that march.

A few weeks later I was walking through Carnhill when I met Jim (Hilter) Breslin, who told me about a token 24-hour hunger strike taking place at the top of Carnhill on Saturday at 12 noon in support of the political prisoners in Crumlin Road Jail. When he asked if I'd like to take part, I immediately said yes, and this was my first involvement with Sinn Féin. Whenever I saw him after that, I always thanked Jim for getting me involved with the party. Later, I joined the local Cumann [branch] in the Shantallow area.

By now, Sinn Féin was organising all the protests and marches in Derry and so I got involved in that type of work and we held marches, protests and pickets against internment in Derry and elsewhere. The chairperson of the party in Shantallow was Jim Kyle, Jim Breslin was the organiser, and Davy Collins the Publicity Officer There was always loads to keep us busy, with other duties like collecting money for the men on the run and the Prisoners' Dependants' Fund. We ran the odd concert in the old Cameo dance hall to raise funds too.

I remember one concert when Eamonn and Kathleen Largey's republican group, The Flying Column, came to perform just after Walker's Pillar was demolished by the IRA. The 96-foot-high pillar used to be on the city walls above the Bogside, with Governor Walker's imposing statue on top. "One of

Orangeism's precious symbols of Protestant Ascendancy in an overwhelmingly Catholic city," is how the Derry Journal described it.

Anyway, the Flying Column travelled all over Ireland performing during the 1970s, and Kathleen was thought of as one of the country's finest ballad singers. What a night that was in Derry, though - with Whitey O'Neill and Eamonn Largey singing Sam Hall, Boolavogue (Father Murphy), and his wife Kathleen singing Four Green Fields. Whitey O'Neill did a lot of fundraising for republican prisoners and the hunger strikers over the years, as did his brother, Junior O'Neill. The entire O'Neill family were great supporters of the republican struggle and still are, though we sadly lost Whitey RIP.

In those days all Cumann [local branch] and Comhairle Ceantair, meetings were held in individual members' homes. The only designated centre in the city was 15 Cable Street, and it was here that the PDF and prisoners' meetings were held. It was important to look after those who might be on the run as well as the prisoners and their families. People just needed support. Eugene (Sauce) Bradley, Eamonn (Lefty) Kelly and I worked for the prisoners until their release under the Good Friday Agreement. We never missed a week in all those years supporting them and the families affected.

With so many personalities involved, things could get heated too. I remember one Comhairle Ceantair meeting in Jim Breslin's house as one debate became argumentative. Barney McFadden was in the chair when Jim argued a point using certain words that Barney didn't like – so Barney told Jim to leave the meeting and go home. Jim then got up and left the meeting, but as he got to the back door, he realised it was his house! "You can't put me out of my own house!" he shouted to Barney, and we all laughed.

When I first got involved with Sinn Féin, I met so many people who were truly dedicated to what they were doing, and seeing passion like that spurred me on too. People like Bobby Sheerin, Patrick (Pudger) O'Hagan, John Coyle, Mary Starrs from the Brandywell, Mrs McNaught, Mrs Daly, Peggy McLaughlin and Ann Starrs from Creggan, and so many others, all working for the prisoners and their families.

It was at these prisoners' meetings that I first met Mitchel McLaughlin who, after the Good Friday Agreement, became a Sinn Féin MLA at Stormont, and later, the first nationalist Speaker of the Northern Ireland Assembly, which we as Republicans in the city and throughout the North were very proud of.

I also got to know Joe McGlinchey after his release from internment and he was one of the most decent people I've ever met. Joe was never shy of putting his hand in his pocket to help the families of fellow prisoners.

Barney McFadden was one of the greatest persons one could be friends with. Although he was older than we were, we always felt safe and secure with Barney and we could depend on him, no matter what the issue. Barney was an all-rounder involved in many branches throughout the republican movement. He was also a member of the GAA and refereed games as well as playing. His wife Roisin was a camogie player, too. I also met for the first time Richard Halpenny and Beatie Barrett was some crack at meetings

In the early 1970s, the Roads Service in Derry was considering building a Flyover along the Lecky Road, and as part of their initial plans they wanted to knock down Free Derry Corner. Barney McFadden wouldn't hear of it, and he protested and protested until they reconsidered and gave in, sparing Free Derry Corner in their final plans. Another good deed by Barney that few people remember.

I got to know Mark and Bella McLaughlin over the years, too, and often visited their home. Mark was the treasurer of Sinn Féin, and a truer republican would be hard to find. I can see where his family got their devout republicanism from, I was honoured to be part of the Guard of Honour at Mark and Bella funerals too.

Mark and Bella were well known as active supporters of the civil rights movement from the 1960s onwards. One of the 50th civil rights exhibitions featured them recently and their role during Free Derry. By then, Mark McLaughlin was an older man, but apparently, he still did his bit during the Battle of the Bogside - by ferrying wheelbarrows full of fresh stones and pebbles back and forth to the rioters at the barricades!

I also became great friends with Willie Hogan and his wife, Sadie, who ran the Prisoners' Dependants' Fund Shop in William Street. Both Willie and Sadie were long-time republicans and worked for the movement until they fell into bad health. They were the salt of the earth and will always be remembered by republicans in Derry.

* * *

The situation in the city deteriorated from 1972 onwards. Not one day passed without hearing about harassment, riots, shootings or gun battles between the IRA and the Brits. On March 14 1972, two unarmed volunteers were shot dead in Dove Gardens by British soldiers. The deaths of these teenagers, 19-year-old

Colm Keenan and 18-year-old Eugene McGillan, stirred yet more resentment towards the British from many of the city's population. Sean MacStiofain gave the graveside oration at Colm's funeral in front of a crowd of thousands.

While many of those first interned in August 1971 had been released, the British army continued to lift others across the North and hold them without trial or a shred of evidence. With hundreds still being interned and army harassment getting steadily worse, the early seventies were full of activity.

Sometimes we protestors took over buildings and banks, going inside them until we were moved on. We'd decide what that day's protest would be, then go take over a local bank with banners and things. Once the cops came on the scene and told us to get out, we got out. We didn't fight them – it was civil disobedience and making ourselves heard. Before that, everything was done under the guise of the civil rights movement, but the whole movement felt destroyed after Bloody Sunday.

The first Bloody Sunday anniversary march in 1973 was organised by Northern Ireland Civil Rights Association, and the second anniversary was organised by both NICRA and us, Sinn Féin. The third anniversary march was completely organised entirely by Sinn Féin and that continued into the mid-1980s when it was handed over to the families.

I was a part of that early organisation alongside people like Barney McFadden, John Johnston and Martha McClelland. I often helped organise marches in general, like the Easter Sunday marches too. Barney McFadden was one of those lifted and interned and when word of his internment spread through Derry, people went were furious because he was so highly thought of in the community.

Gerry McCartney was once telling me about his time interned in Long Kesh, and how Barney McFadden was considered an inspiration to other young internees in the Kesh. Despite being one of the oldest internees in there, on the night the Kesh burned, and the army battled, gassed and battered internees, Barney apparently gave back as much as he got and never backed down.

*

By summer of 1972, the political pressure to sort out the North's no-go areas was building, and so the British army planned a massive invasion operation – Operation Motorman – for July 31 that year. The plan was to regain control and smash all the no-go areas – including Free Derry.

Over 21,000 troops were sent in on the morning of Motorman, making it the single biggest British military operation since the Second World War. People were worried, and rightly so. The IRA – outnumbered against an entire army – decided to leave the no-go areas but it made no difference. The Brits still caused chaos coming in and two people were dead by nightfall.

On the morning of Motorman, I was elsewhere as one of my friends, John Hutton, got married to Angela Gallagher and I was his best man. With all the army in the city, we had considerable difficulty getting to the chapel and the reception afterwards in the Broom Hill Hotel. We did eventually get there, but we had to walk it back into the city centre afterwards, and when we got there the city was saturated with armed Brits and tanks. It was a war zone. Motorman must have cost the Road Service a fortune too as the army's Centurion tanks and armoured vehicles literally broke up and destroyed roads and footpaths all over town.

I remember that we had to walk in single file going over the Craigavon Bridge that night because it was all blocked off. We needed a pass to get through, which the hotel had given us, and shortly afterwards John and Angela went off on their honeymoon. Our friend Barney Kelly was at the wedding too, and a few months later he would be shot dead in Annie's Bar.

The army caused chaos while we were at that wedding and Motorman became a day that nobody would ever forget. A local Volunteer, Seamus Bradley, and a younger schoolboy, Daniel Hegarty, were both shot dead by the army in highly controversial circumstances. Their families spent decades since, looking for truth and justice. Daniel Hegarty was only fifteen, and the army shot him twice in the head at point-blank range when he was out innocently watching the tanks coming in. They said afterwards that he was a gunman, which was just lies. Seamus Bradley was unarmed when the army shot him five times and left him to die of his injuries. The Claudy bombing happened later the same day. It was a terrible event for the people there.

1972 ended up being the worst year of the Troubles with the highest number of deaths in that one year as so many people lost their lives.

We lost yet more IRA Volunteers at the hands of the Brits from 1972 to 1974, too. Men and women like Volunteers John Starrs, Michael Quigley, John Brady, James Carr, James (Junior) McDaid, Joe Walker, Gerard Craig, David Russell, Michael Meenan, John McDaid, and Ethel Lynch. Junior McDaid was the first O.C. (Officer Commanding) of the 3rd Battalion Derry Brigade and the first Volunteer to be killed by the army in our area of Shantallow.

One of our closest friends, Barney Kelly, was shot dead by the UDA loyalist gang who attacked Annie's Bar in Top of the Hill in the Waterside in December

1972. They were in the bar watching a football match when the UDA burst in with a submachine gun and a pistol, killing five people including Barney. It was such a terrible night when it came on the news, and we heard he was among the dead. It was devastating for all their families, and for us. We were always great friends, going to the dances together and meeting up for drinks on our holidays. Barney had been at the same wedding as us the day of Operation Motorman.

I met another friend of mine, Terry Francis, at the Collon Bar in the mid-1970s. It was a great bar and a great bunch of people you could meet; at the weekends we would have the crack especially on a Saturday night you would have Terry, Robbie, Ciaran McColgan with his (six pints at the end of the night) tabs, Jerry Bradley, Willie (the Yank) Gallagher, Big Joe Long and Frankie O'Neill, who helped look after the Prisoners' Dependants' Fund and collected donations in the bar at the weekends.

Around June 1974, there was some talk that internment might be coming to an end, but the talk came to nothing as young men and women were still being lifted all the time and held without reason.

In November 1974, several men from our part of Shantallow were lifted and interned, including Jim Breslin who was – at the time - the chairperson of Shantallow Sinn Féin. Jim Kyle, Davey Collins, John Oakley, Frankie O'Neill and a few others were taken too. This left Neil McLaughlin and me at the forefront of the leadership in the Shantallow area.

It really was incredible just how one-sided internment was in terms of which communities were being targeted and harassed by the British. Of the 1,981 people interned since Operation Demetrius began with Ballymurphy in 1971 until it ended in December 1975, only 107 were loyalists and 1,874 were republican or nationalist. It seems unbelievable that this was allowed to happen in modern society – and yet it was.

There were more rumours of a truce between the British and the IRA, and a ceasefire was announced from Sunday 22 December 1974 until 2 January 1975. I think those involved held out a hope that the British would agree to withdraw from the North. It never happened.

Closer to home on 13 January 1975, Volunteer James Moyne died in Long Kesh because of medical neglect, and it was a terribly sad time for his family and comrades and another reason for growing frustration among us.

* * *

During the restarted IRA/British truce that went from 10 February until summer 1976, Sinn Féin members were asked to set up seven official incident centres to monitor the ceasefire and the actions of the British army on the ground.

A meeting was held in Jim's house in Carnhill, and a senior republican met with Jim, Bobby Sheerin and Neil McLaughlin and me as we needed to find premises for an incident centre and quickly. Neil and I were tasked with finding a suitable building in the Shantallow area, and although we looked for a few days - we could only manage to get a caravan that had been permanently sat at Shantallow shops beside the Post Office.

The caravan had no lighting which made it pretty useless in the evenings. Because we needed it open until 10pm each night, Jim McGilloway who lived beside the caravan, a man I knew well, got in touch offering help and said that we could run an extension from his house to the caravan for electricity. This was agreed, and we were able to keep the office open till 10pm. I must say that the extension lead stayed attached from 1975-1983 when we moved the office, which was very good of them considering.

The same family accepted food parcels for the political prisoners in their home for delivery to the Crum and Long Kesh and collected by the PDF bus every week. This continued until all prisoners were released. For these reasons and more, the republican movement holds Jim, Jean and their family in high esteem for all the work and help they gave to our struggle. This was acknowledged at the Annual Republican Volunteers Dinner Dance later on.

The Shantallow incident centre was staffed by republicans and Sinn Féin members from 10am until 10pm, and we monitored all the movements of the British army. People like Nan Quigley, Molly Kavanagh, Margaret Harkin and Margo McLaughlin worked there steadily for over three months. These great women, and others like Bridget McDaid, Mary Breslin, Loretta Kelly and Marion McGilloway were the backbone of republicanism in the 1970s in the Shantallow and Carnhill areas. People never forget just how much they gave to the republican movement over the years.

We monitored all the army's actions. How many times they patrolled, how many times they stopped people, where the locations were, and so on. The incident centre was open from 10am until 10pm at night. We would get notified about people being stopped by the army, which would happen on a daily basis, and we always had a team at the centre there who would drive straight there to help and to bring the man or woman who was being stopped

We physically got involved and helped people rather than just advising them. This was all before computers and we had no typewriters, so we had triplicate sheets where we recorded everything like the details of the incident, what it was about and its location, and every day someone from within the movement went around the various incident centres gathering copies of each incident report. The main representatives who did the negotiating with the Brits would then take these cases to the army asking them to sort it out.

During that time, we could legitimately ask the army, "What's your name?" and if a soldier protested, we told them, "We are reporting you to the main incident centre in the city." It was great for those couple of months because we could tell the Brits to get to fuck! It didn't last long though as the truce broke around July that year and then we all ran for cover!

One afternoon, Bobby Sheerin, a few others and I were in the centre when a British army major, Major Brown, came to the door and addressed Bobby as Councillor Sheerin in Irish! That surprised all of us – here was a major in the British army being a fluent Irish speaker and imagine us not understanding him! He said his family were from Cork.

The monitoring centres were really a precursor to the advice centres that were set up a few years later. From then on, we operated advice centres in Shantallow, Creggan, the Bogside and even the Waterside.

The IRA ceasefire began and ended a few times. It was renewed on February 10 and lasted until that summer of 1975, when the IRA realised the British had no intentions of withdrawing from the North. Things had returned to the way they were before. That July, we got news that internees might be released, and the then-Secretary of state Merlyn Rees even suggested they could be out by Christmas, but few believed him. We were right.

* * *

Little by little, internees had been slowly released from wherever they were held. On Friday December 5, 1975, Merlyn Rees announced the official end of internment in the North, and the last forty-six internees were let out. I remember Gerry Fitt, the leader of the SDLP party at the time, thought that ending internment would "take away the greatest emotional weapon that the Provisional IRA ever had."

Despite the end of internment, all was not rosy in the North. Soon another, more serious chapter in our history would begin because of another British mistake – their decision to criminalise our political prisoners. When the Secretary of State Merlyn Rees first declared his intention to withdraw prisoners' Special Category Status during a speech in November 1975, few imagined the impact this would have. Within months it would lead to the Blanket and No Wash protests in the H-Blocks, which led to the later Hunger Strikes and men dying for their country - and the British government in deep water for allowing it to happen.

CHAPTER 11
The Prison Protests

After the 1975 truce ended, the rest of the year played out as before but this time it got worse as the proposed new British policy of criminalising our political prisoners began to cause problems in Long Kesh and Crumlin Road jail.

Tragedy hit the Breslin family in Carnhill when Jim's six-year-old son Kevin was knocked down by a car just yards from his own home. I remember it was such a terrible time for the family and the whole community.

The same month Tommy McGlinchey was attacked by loyalists UVF/UDA when they planted a bomb in his car outside his home at Chapel Road. The car exploded when he started it, causing him to lose both legs - and still Tommy remained a republican activist until the day he died. His friend and comrade Jim McCafferty came under fire from the same loyalist gang when he was in a car with another man driving towards Top of the Hill in the Waterside, and they had a lucky escape with their lives.

In late 1975, a new Sinn Féin Comhairle Ceantair was formed, and Barney McFadden was elected to the position of Chair. Barney was earlier released from Long Kesh, and I was proposed as vice chair of the Comhairle Ceantair.

Among the first decisions we took on was when the Chair proposed to run a Christmas postal service and that any money raised as a result would go to the Prisoners' Dependants' Fund. Of course, Johnny Johnston, Martha McClelland and I agreed straight away.

The first stamp that we issued as part of our Christmas Postal Service featured an image of the General Post Office in Dublin as it burned during the Rising in Easter 1916. Every year after that, the stamp reflected contemporary events and we kept informed of what was happening at that time, like the Hunger Strikes and the blanket protests. We felt it important to have a strong political message on the stamp every year.

It was very amusing when we heard that the British MP, William Ross, made an official complaint to Westminster about Sinn Féin running a postal service in Derry. He said publicly that we were undermining the postal service in the city, and that action should be taken against the party to stop it. In response, the Post Office came out publicly to say that no action would be taken, as the Sinn Féin post would not affect postal service in Derry. The Sinn Féin Christmas

Post lasted for years after that, with the last one carried out in 2019.

In 2015, a German scholar called Heinz-Jurgen Kumpf came to Derry to do some research on the subject of our unique postal service, and he later wrote a book about it all. The book included research and interviews from me and images of some of the stamps over the years. I hear it's now in a lot of libraries in Europe.

Over the next few years and throughout the 1970s, problems in Long Kesh and Crumlin Road jail escalated with prisoners frequently being beaten and ill-treated by prison officers.

Back home, their families and communities were furious that the British and Irish government had turned a blind eye to such abusive behaviour, and H-Block Committees were set up to protest on behalf of the prisoners. In Derry, women including Mary Nelis, Martha McClelland and Daisy Mules became vocal and powerful activists, campaigning tirelessly for prisoners' rights. If I recall correctly, one protest involved Mary Nelis and a few other local mothers protesting in a blanket outside the Bishop of Derry's house! Despite Derry's awful weather, they wore only blankets around them in solidarity with their jailed sons.

For a time, there were regular protests both inside and outside the prisons, all aimed at highlighting the plight of political prisoners. One remarkable Derry woman, Kathleen Gallagher, gave her life in support of the political prisoners - visiting every prison in the country.

In Shantallow, Neil McLaughlin and I were often the front-runners in terms of organising and overseeing Sinn Féin activity in the area. Neil was the Sinn Féin Organiser for the party and would later spend years travelling all over the country spreading its word. The caravan that we used as an incident centre during the 1975 truce was still there outside Shantallow Shops, and so we decided to open an advice centre to deal with problems in the community. We held a meeting of the Cumann where it was decided to ask Bobby Kelly to staff the centre.

As we had recommissioned the old Sinn Féin caravan, we were able to hold some Cumann meetings there. One night a meeting started slightly early and old Joe Cool was last in and so sat with his back to the doorway. Suddenly, a load of Brits appeared at the caravan door and started asking us all for our names, which we had no doubt they knew already. Old Joe was the first to be asked, and he point-blank refused to tell the soldier his name, so we all had to follow Joe and refused to identify ourselves, which, of course, caused chaos and the Brits overreacted and radioed for support. Before we knew it, the caravan was surrounded by army land rovers, and we were all lifted and taken to Fort George where we were held for four hours. Ha ha! Joe never did give his name.

We were relieved to get out that night, but the bigger problem was that Shantallow House was closed, and we didn't get a pint that night of all nights! Either way, Joe would be top table at any meetings in future.

* * *

The Shantallow advice centre was open five days a week and dealt with all sorts of complaints and queries from the local community. We had different members tasked with specific complaints, and I would take care of any housing issues. Tony Devine and Bobby Sheerin oversaw any protest issues and street problems, and Eamon 'Lefty' Kelly would cover the caravan shifts at night-times, along with John McCool who was a veteran republican and one of the best fundraisers I ever met.

Housing complaints in particular took up a lot of our time. The Housing Executive office was nearby at the top of Carnhill, and the area manager at that time was Paddy McIntyre who, of course, we tortured about housing problems all the time. Paddy later became Chief Executive of the entire Housing Executive, and I met him on many more occasions years later during my time as a Sinn Féin Councillor for Derry before he sadly passed away.

One of the most dramatic assassinations of the whole conflict occurred on October 28, 1976 when Maire Drumm, a woman I greatly admired, was shot dead by a loyalist death squad in a Belfast hospital. She was vice-president of Sinn Féin at the time and her murder quite rightly made headline news across the world. Drumm had been a thorn in the side of the British crown forces, and often courted serious harassment for her stance against what she saw as the occupation of part of Ireland by a foreign power.

The attack itself was shockingly blatant, with two gunmen dressed as hospital doctors entering the grounds of the Mater Hospital and making it up to Maire Drumm's hospital bed before opening fire and hitting her three times before fleeing. Rioting erupted in Belfast as she was such a well-known leader and a woman. Belfast and Derry were in turmoil. The fact that the attackers could go into a hospital dressed as doctors to shoot her without being detected proved collusion without a doubt. I often wondered, why weren't some of our own people there keeping guard? In the years after that, people were inclined to be there outside the door as protection when a prominent republican was in hospital. When Martin McGuinness went into hospital, there were often half a dozen people there as a presence to ensure he wasn't interfered with.

* * *

In 1976, the British government declared that the North's political prisoners would no longer be entitled to Special Category status. In other words, the prisoners were now considered 'ordinary criminals' – a decision that had far-reaching consequences for many. The new policy came into effect on March 1, 1976, and we organised protests in support of the prisoners which led to riots and unrest in the streets. I was part of the crowd there on the streets certainly – we were always there to swell the crowd and show support. There were also mad rioters there too, of course. The funny thing about people rioting here was that they often rioted with a shirt and tie and suit on – smartly dressed rioters! In those days, we would put on a shirt and tie even going out to play darts or to the pictures.

We lost two more Volunteers in 1976, which was another huge blow not just to their families but to the movement. On 17 May 1976, Jim Gallagher was shot dead by British soldiers as he sat on a bus on his way home – just days away from his 21st birthday. I read a story by one of his sisters and in it she said that they had bought lots of fancy food for his 21st party and it ended up being used for his wake.

On 30 June, Vol. Brian Coyle was killed in a grenade attack against the British army in Meenan Square in the city's Bogside. Every time we lost someone in the movement, it was a terrible blow and hard to cope with. It was a struggle. We found a way, I suppose.

The 'Blanket Protest' started in September 1976, when Kieran Nugent became the first man sentenced under the new criminal status – and then the first to refuse to wear a prison uniform. From there, things got worse, and the treatment of the blanket men was punishment each day in itself.

Barney McFadden started a weekly protest in support of the prisoners which went on for months. Every Saturday at 3pm we gathered near the old public toilets in Waterloo Square. Barney would be there with a big crowd surrounding him as he read out all the latest news from the 'Kesh' and 'Crum'. Every week without fail, Alex O'Donnell and John O'Hagan would bring the posters to the protest.

Protesting increased in 1978 as word got out that prisoners were refusing to leave their cells to shower because of attacks by prison officers. This ultimately led to the Hunger Strikes, and behind it all was the British government. That year we lost another three Volunteers too, Vol. Dennis Heaney in June, Vol. Pat Harkin in October, and Vol. Patsy Duffy in November.

The Sinn Féin Advice Office in Shantallow managed by Bobby Kelly was working really well, with quite a few people using it when they needed help and advice. Despite it being such a necessary resource within the community, the British army paid the caravan office plenty of visits in the early hours of the morning. I've no doubt the army were determined to see it demolished, and they did cause deliberate damage on a few occasions. Every time it was damaged republicans in the area rallied around for support, led by people like Mickey McLaughlin, Alec O'Donnell, John O'Hagan and big Phil McGilloway.

When the boys and Big Phil fixed the damage, he put the national flag back on top of the caravan which really antagonised the passing Brits patrols. We could always rely on those comrades when we needed them.

CHAPTER 12
The Hunger Strike

By early 1979, the streets of Derry and other places across the North seemed to erupt daily with prison protests. We knew if the Brits didn't give in to prisoners' demands soon, they risked further escalation of these protests, both inside and outside of the prison system.

I think we all quietly hoped that a solution would be found, but as months passed with little response from the British, it became clear just how little Irish lives mattered – and just how bad the situation could get.

The Hunger Strike started on October 28, 1980, when seven prisoners refused food – among them Derry man Raymond McCartney.

Raymond was from a well-known republican family in Derry, and his mother, father and brothers were all involved in the movement. He had gone to jail very early on and spent years inside for something he didn't do, alongside another Derry man, Eamonn MacDermott. He and MacDermott were lifted and charged with shooting an RUC Detective Constable in a garage on the Strand Road in 1979. They both served seventeen years for it and in 2007, decades later and long after their release, their conviction was quashed, and they were exonerated. Raymond has been a republican icon in this city, both for his role in the Hunger Strikes and later, as a politician.

When Raymond went on hunger strike, we were all behind him as a Derry man. The same with Patsy O'Hara and Mickey Devine. We were behind them all.

The initial hunger strike went on for fifty-three days, when a compromise was made that the men could wear their own clothes. With this compromise agreed, the prisoners ended their hunger strike in the belief they'd be getting their own clothes back. Families brought clothing into the prison in readiness, but of course, the British government had other plans. We just didn't know it yet.

I was at a H-Block meeting in the Shantallow Community Centre when word came through that the only clothes the prisoners could expect were special prison issue uniforms. This was clearly not what prisoners had been told. They'd double-crossed us. Once again, the British government had failed to live up to an agreement – and the realisation of this caused fury and anger both inside and outside of the prisons. The men went off the hunger strike as soon as they were told they could wear their own clothes – that's what saved Raymond's life.

Soon we heard another hunger strike was being considered. This was something the republican leadership didn't want, because if the British could lie about the so-called deal, it was felt that Margaret Thatcher would let them die.

In a statement, the republican prisoners warned of further hunger strikes unless they were awarded Special Category Status by the British government. The government refused. That's when another hunger strike was decided on, and Bobby Sands, felt that because he was Commanding Officer of IRA prisoners in Long Kesh that it was his duty to lead it. Bobby began refusing food and so began a new hunger strike on 1 March 1981. This course of action would end in the death of ten prisoners.

Around the same time in March 1981, the Independent MP for Fermanagh and South Tyrone, Frank Maguire, died suddenly, with his death prompting a by-election. The H-Block committee, the organisation that lobbied for prisoners' rights, nominated Bobby Sands as a candidate for the constituency. No other nationalist candidate would stand, so Bobby got a free run and won the election, polling over 30,400 votes despite being incarcerated.

Sadly, it wouldn't last long as Thatcher did not give in and she let Bobby die. Thatcher did everything to put the Irish people down. She's responsible for the hunger strikers, for shoot to kill policies and collusion. Within a year of the hunger strikes the situation in the H-Blocks was eased, so why did she allow men to die?

Bobby Sands died on May 5, 1981, after sixty-six days on hunger strike. He was only 27 years old. In the weeks and months afterwards, more of his comrades followed.

The New York Times reported on Bobby Sands and the many protests that occurred internationally after his death on hunger strike. Over a thousand protestors marched on the British Embassy in Athens. In Oslo, the British monarch was jeered arriving for a four-day visit, and in Moscow, the official Soviet press agency reported that Sands had died in what was basically a British concentration camp. An Australian politician said Thatcher's actions had brought the North to crisis point, and demonstrators poured mock blood on a British flag in Brisbane, before delivering it to the British High Commission offices there. The first street named after Bobby Sands was in Cuba, and there are now streets and places in America and around the world named after him, that's how big an impact he had.

Within our own community we needed a way to mark the passing of any hunger strikers and so a siren was fitted to the Sinn Féin caravan in Shantallow for this very reason. Philip McGilloway was in charge of it, and when the death of a hunger striker happened, he would sound the siren, calling people up to the caravan. When they got there, someone was there to inform them about any local protests being organised and how people could show their support and solidarity.

The fact that Sands was elected was massive and it put the republican cause into a new category where it could be heard through politics. There was a feeling that if Bobby could do it, they could too. It offered an alternative, and I think that was the start of the gradual move towards politics. Never should we forget them: Bobby Sands, Francis Hughes, Ray McCree, Patsy O'Hara, Joe McDonnell, Martin Hurson, Kevin Lynch, Kieran Doherty, Tom McElwee and Mickey Devine.

We'll also remember Michael Gaughan, who died on 3 June 1974, and Frank Stagg on 12 May 1976, and all the other republicans who gave their lives on hunger strike from the 1920s to the present day.

* * *

As Bobby Sands was an MP, his death brought about another by-election and Owen Carron was selected to run as he had been Bobby's election agent. He was elected with an increased majority, and as a H-Block candidate he didn't take his seat at Westminster.

The election of Bobby and Owen led to a debate within Sinn Féin and the movement in general about the benefits of fighting future elections and how it would advance the struggle. The debate went on for months, with some believing the political route was worth pursuing, and others highly sceptical.

Because of the political deadlock, there had been talks of establishing a new assembly, and that Sinn Féin should get involved. Meetings after meetings were held all over the place to gauge opinion and support, and finally it was agreed to fight the Assembly Election if one were called. Martin McGuinness was proposed as the Derry candidate, with Cathal Crumley running with him.

The Assembly election was called on 20 October 1982, and Sinn Féin contested as themselves gaining a total party vote of over 64,000 across the North. In Derry itself, Martin McGuinness won over 8,000 votes. Gerry Adams, Owen Carron, Danny Morrison, and Jim McAllister were also elected, but didn't take their seats in the assembly. More than anything, the election results showed the swell of support for Sinn Féin that now existed in the community.

Soon after the assembly election, a number of Sinn Féin members were called to a special meeting of Derry Comhairle Ceantair for a debate on the coming 1985 local government council elections. For years and years beforehand, the local district body was called Londonderry City Council, but its name was changed to Derry City Council in 1984. Today it incorporates Strabane too, becoming Derry City and Strabane District Council, which is shortened to DCSDC on paper.

Anyway, ahead of the local elections, Neil McLaughlin and I were asked to explore the Shantallow area to find out how Sinn Féin would fare if we put candidates forward. We talked to several people in Shantallow who had worked for the old Nationalist party and withdrew from the new Irish Independence Party, people like Tommy Mitchell, who gave his life to the pursuit of Catholic registration and ensuring the Catholic population got their voting rights.

After we consulted the community, Neil and I met Bobby Sheerin in Jim Breslin's house in Shantallow to discuss our findings before presenting them to the Derry Comhairle Ceantair. We were advised we could run two or three candidates for our area and probably get two elected. Other areas did the same to find out how much support Sinn Féin had in the city, and after debate and public feedback, it was agreed that the party would take part in the May 1985 council elections.

It was now a question of selecting the right candidates, and the party in Shantallow put several potential names forward. A Selection Committee was agreed upon to look at the names and make decisions. Swayed by our findings and recommendations, they collectively decided to run three candidates for local council and Gerry Doherty, Susie O'Hagan and Liam McCartney were nominated.

Gerry McCartney was proposed as director of the election and almost immediately he formed an Election Committee to get things done! When the campaign started, we canvassed the streets endlessly and must have knocked on every door in every area, calling on people to give us their vote. The campaign went really well, and when the local council elections were eventually held, Gerry Doherty was elected for Shantallow and Liam McCartney lost by 27 votes, just as we had predicted. In all, Sinn Féin got five councillors elected to council that year, Barney McFadden, Mitchel McLaughlin, Hugh Brady, Dodie McGuinness, and Gerry Doherty, as well as having a representative in the Assembly. This in my view was the start of growth in the party in the city.

Naturally, we now had to provide a constituency service in the city and the wee caravan in Shantallow was far from an appropriate office! The pressure was on to find another, more suitable premises to set up. Pat Coyle was the Sinn Féin organiser at the time and found a site at Delvin's shopping complex beside Shantallow House that would make an ideal space for the community.

From here, Councillor Gerry Doherty ran his constituency office in the heart of the community. I remember John Doherty was appointed to take over the security of the office, which was necessary because we still had the ongoing problems with loyalist gangs in the city.

Although politics was now active in the city, the republican movement was steadily losing Volunteers, killed while either on active duty or as civilians, unarmed and unaware. The bigoted, brutal RUC were known to behave disgracefully during republican funerals, showing harassment and blind contempt for every one of us. I remember they behaved particularly badly during the funerals of Volunteers Willie Fleming, Paddy Deery and Eddie McSheffrey. That's how cold they were, they'd deliberately upset and disrupt a grieving community and heartbroken families without a second thought.

My home at Moss Park was raided a number of times by the RUC and British army and I was lifted by the police and army on a number of occasions. Ciaran and Áine were fairly young, thankfully. There was one time during a raid that Áine was a baby in the cot, a Brit said, "Lift that baby out of the cot!" so they could search it. I was always vigilant and waiting for the next raid when you knew they were out raiding. There would be times with hardly any raids but if there was, you tended to wake earlier in the mornings and be more on guard.

As the Troubles raged through the 1980s, many innocent civilians were killed - men, women and children. Our list of fallen comrades also grew. Among the Republican Movement, we lost many on active service between May 1981 and October 1987, fifteen men in total. These were Volunteer George McBrearty (May 28 1981), Vol. Charles Maguire (May 28 1981), Vol. Eamonn Bradley (August 25 1982), Vol. Phil O'Donnell (December 24, 1982), Vol. Richard Quigley (April 21, 1984), Vol. Ciaran Fleming (December 2, 1984), Vol. Danny Doherty (December 6, 1984), Vol. Willie Fleming (December 6, 1984), Vol. Charles English (August 6, 1985), Vol. Tony Gough (February 22, 1986), Vol. Philip McFadden (May 31, 1986), Vol. Patrick O'Hagan (August 9, 1986), Vol. Gerard Logue (March 22, 1987), Vol. Paddy Deery (October 28, 1987) and Vol. Eddie McSheffrey (October 28, 1987).

One experience that stands out is when we were burying Vol. Willie Fleming in December 1984. His entire funeral was blocked and obstructed by the RUC from the Waterside to the City side – they were relentless. We carried his coffin all over the city with the national flag atop for everyone to see. It was late on a dark evening when we finally reached the republican plot of the City Cemetery for burial. On a hill overlooking the whole city, our cemetery might be one of the most picturesque resting places around.

Similar scenes were caused during the funerals of Vol. Paddy Deery and Vol. Eddie McSheffrey when RUC officers laid in wait and literally attacked the funeral party and family. They forced the coffin to the ground. I still can't believe they did that – just imagine the disrespect needed to attack a funeral. The anger towards the RUC was almost palpable.

CHAPTER 13
The Assassination of Bronco

Volunteer Eamonn 'Bronco' Bradley was only 23 years-old and unarmed when the British army assassinated him in cold blood. It happened on 25 August 1982, behind the Shantallow House near where he lived. He clearly caused no threat to the Brits, but they shot him dead anyway.

Bronco was a personal friend, as was his whole family. He was a good-looking guy, always well-dressed and he liked to look after his hair. He was also very sincere and happy to help out when needed, like when the Brits damaged the advice centre, or we needed support. It was shocking to hear what happened.

I was in the Shantallow Sinn Féin caravan that day when someone came in looking for a lift to a meeting, and off we went. On the way we saw Brits everywhere and some kind of commotion outside Shantallow House. Naturally, we went the other way and away from the direction of the Brits, but it later turned out the crowd was about Bronco.

He had been coming out of Shantallow house where he'd been playing a game of pool. An army foot patrol coming up the road eyeballed him and called for him to halt, but before he could even halt, they fired. Hearing the shots, Bobby Sheerin who was working in the bar ran out to his assistance, but Bronco was already dead.

Just weeks before, his friends were lifted by the army and their interrogators warned them that they would shoot Bronco. "We'll nail Bronco," they threatened – and they did. They shot him in the back. A lot of people saw or heard this happen and it's a small, tight community so people were rightly shaken up and annoyed at what had happened.

Bronco's mother never got over his death until the day she died. He was buried with full republican honours in the City Cemetery, and I was honoured to have chaired the graveside proceedings. As I recall, Sean Keenan gave the oration and Johnny O'Hagan played the Last Post at the graveside.

Like so many others we'd lost, Bronco was much loved and respected locally and further afield. So well thought of, in fact, that a group of us republicans met together to pool ideas on how best keep Bronco's memory alive. From then on it was decided to host an annual quiz night from Bronco's first anniversary onwards. The quiz had a special trophy cup donated by pub manager Bobby

Sheerin of Shantallow House. Sometime later Martin (Gills) McGilloway suggested the idea of an annual football competition in his honour. That first year, the inaugural Eamonn (Bronco) Bradley Seven-a-Side Final was won by Shantallow Youth Club.

As interest and popularity grew, a committee of individuals were charged with overseeing commemorative events which included Vinny Barr, Owen Boyle and the late Jackie McFadden. We were amazed at how popular the Bronco events became every year, with more and more teams signing up. One of the main hurdles for us was trying to get sponsorship for events. We really wanted to give cash prizes to winning teams, but for this, of course, you need good sponsors.

A new committee explored possibilities of extra funding, and that new group including myself, Oliver McFadden, Peter McDonald, Terry Francis, Jim Breslin and Bobby Sheerin. We got busy contacting various people and organisations and managed to get more funding for the competition. The main sponsorship of the whole competition was Martin Sheehan of K.S. Electrics, and he remains the primary sponsor today almost twenty years later.

With additional funding available, the committee decided to add the late Vol. Dennis Heaney to the competition too as there were many similarities in how the Brits killed Dennis and Bronco. So we renamed the competition the Bronco/ Heaney Memorial Cup in memory of the two Volunteers and it still runs annually today.

All credit and thanks go to the Bradley and Heaney families for allowing and trusting us to run the competition all these years in memory of Bronco and Dennis. None of which would have been possible without Martin McGilloway, who has hosted the competition all these years.

* * *

As the years passed, the Sinn Féin offices in the city grew busier and busier in terms of constituency work. By this time, Mitchel McLaughlin was chairperson of Derry Sinn Féin, and, for the first time, we felt hope in being a strong political party determined to serve those who voted us in.

Simultaneously, the North's Dept. of Health and Social Security (DHSS) were forced to implement a better benefit take-up scheme for NI citizens after it emerged that people with serious health issues were not getting their full benefit entitlement or the information needed to make such decisions. Back then, Eugene Bradley was considered one of the best welfare rights officers in the city. Leading a team in the Shantallow area, he succeeded in getting hundreds of people their money back when needed – and even backdated their money whenever he could.

Sinn Féin had another two local council elections between 1989-1993, as well as two Westminster elections between 1983-1987, with Adams winning the two Westminster elections. Closer to home, Gerry Doherty didn't want to run for council so Gearóid Ó hEára and Ricky Halpenny were selected to run in the 1989 local election, with Ó hEára taking the seat. A few years later in 1993, Pinta McKnight was his running mate, but again Gearóid won and took the council seat. In 1992, Gerry Adams lost his Westminster seat to Joe Hendon. He regained the seat in 1997 and held it until he left and went to the Dáil.

With Mitchel McLaughlin elected to Derry City Council, the local Sinn Féin party needed a new chairperson for the party and Mickey English was appointed. Mickey was a good man. He had two sons killed by the British army, the first his 19 year-old son Gary English who was deliberately struck and killed by a British army armoured vehicle on Easter Sunday 19 April 1981 alongside his friend, Jim Brown. This all took place just outside St Eugene's Cathedral, and Jim Brown, who was just seventeen, was killed instantly on impact. Gary English did not die straight away but as a result of the same Land Rover reversing over him as he lay injured on the road, killing him.

Mickey's other son, Vol. Charles English, died two years later on 6 August 1985, killed by security forces in Abbey Street in the Bogside. He was just 21 years-old.

* * *

As the 20th anniversary of the Battle of the Bogside drew near in 1989, Sinn Féin members met frequently to discuss options and how they could celebrate the defeat of the RUC at last. Among the suggestions put forward for 50th events were a photographic exhibition and a republican concert.

Martin McGuinness suggested a march from Creggan to Free Derry Corner, and while some worried we might not get a crowd, the idea was given the go-ahead. That turned out to be one of the biggest marches seen in Derry since Bloody Sunday in 1972.

Sinn Féin organised the Bloody Sunday anniversary marches in Derry from 1973 onwards, until responsibility for the march was handed over to the Bloody Sunday families in the early 1980s. By the time families had mobilised to take the reins, their long campaign for truth and justice had begun. Little did they know that this grassroots campaign would go on to change British and Irish history forever.

Other republican marches that were held at Easter and June were organised by Barney McFadden; Johnny Johnson and me. Local anniversaries of Volunteers were taking place almost every month too, so a decision was made that the last Sunday in June be used to commemorate all local Volunteers who made the supreme sacrifice in the Derry Brigade. This annual commemoration continues today and is called the Volunteers weekend.

Over the next few years, politics took up a lot of our time on the ground and we really got to know the community and its many characters. We were also aware that some type of talks were taking place behind the scenes, and it wasn't long after that that the party began to debate their new document, A Scenario for Peace, that explored the options and benefits of agreement.

This paper stated that national self-determination had never been relinquished by the Irish people and therefore the Irish people had the right to self-determination, which means there is no reason why the British should maintain their occupation of Ireland.

As the newly appointed chairperson of Sinn Féin for the North, Gearóid Ó hEára was always on the go or travelling to other parts of the North selling the peace process. When he was absent, I stood in for him looking after his constituency work. Gearóid Ó hEára was often joined by Jim Breslin on these journeys, and I can only imagine the political conversations that must have gone on between those two!

By 1990, as Gearóid was away at times, he asked Bridie Coyle to staff the Derry office which worked out well as Bridie stayed in that position for years.

Just beyond Derry into Donegal, a popular Sinn Féin Councillor called Eddie Fullerton was gunned down by loyalist gunmen in his Buncrana home. His murder on 18 May 1991 was believed to have been the work of the Ulster Defence Association (UDA) colluding with the British security services. More recent evidence points to the gunman himself being a British military intelligence agent.

Eddie was a very popular and much-loved character, so his murder was devastating. The huge turn-out for his funeral showed just how well-respected he truly was by the community he served. There was no justice in Eddie Fullerton's case, just like so many others, and there is still a palpable anger in Buncrana over his murder and the lack of accountability.

* * *

Throughout these years, it's important to remember that we also faced the British government's broadcasting ban, which basically censored the voices of prominent republican and loyalist activists on TV and radio. The ban lasted from 1988 until 1994, a long time.

When the ban was first announced we had protests outside BBC Radio Foyle with masks over our mouths to draw attention, and there were other protests all over the North. We kept doing so for years until the ban was lifted. The whole idea was laughable really. They put Gerry Adams on TV with an actor's voice speaking for him like some odd joke, and we rightly protested. We thought it was ridiculous. Why censor someone talking if you're still publicly broadcasting what that person is saying? It just doesn't make any sense. Once again, the Brits learned nothing from their mistakes. They still haven't.

By now it was the early 1990s and talks were starting to happen between John Hume and Gerry Adams – though this fact wasn't publicly known at the time. These secret talks eventually led to the Downing Street Declaration on 15 December 1993, followed nine months later by the IRA announcing a ceasefire on August 31, 1994.

Things seemed quiet for a while after the IRA called its ceasefire, and after several weeks had passed the loyalist groups also called a ceasefire. Their ceasefire statement was read out by Gusty Spence himself - a convicted killer of a Catholic barman in Belfast in 1966.

We had to play our part too, and Jim Breslin, Neil McLaughlin and I were called with other comrades to the Cable Street office to meet the Comhairle Ceantair. We were briefed on the situation and needed to communicate the news. We three planned to walk the length and breadth of our areas to spread the word about the ceasefire announcement.

We spent the rest of that day and night knocking on doors all over Shantallow and speaking to as many republican supporters as we could find. Thankfully, the response to the ceasefire was one-hundred percent positive, and on some doorsteps, we were met with hugs and delight that the war was over. Unfortunately, the IRA ceasefire broke down in February 1996 in response to Sinn Féin being excluded from peace negotiations.

On February 9, 1996 the IRA planted a massive bomb in the London Docklands that exploded and killed two people. The blast caused immense damage to buildings and infrastructure too, with damage costs afterwards estimated at more than £150 million.

That same year, the NI Forum for Political Dialogue was set up with the aim of getting the various parties talking to each other. Sinn Féin gained seventeen seats in the Forum election, but the party remained excluded from talks because of ongoing IRA violence. Throughout that time, we held protests all over the city.

The IRA ceasefire was restored in July 1997, and for a time we enjoyed an unsteady peace. Shortly after the 1994 ceasefire, Sinn Féin got involved in opening roads that the Brits had closed off years before for security reasons. The army insisted they were going to reopen some of these roads, but any they chose were roads that didn't go anywhere and didn't matter to the community. This was the reason why Sinn Féin decided to act themselves to reopen roads that were actually used and needed by the community.

This coordinated action involved Sinn Féin members and local border action committees getting involved. In the Derry area, we reopened roads at Lenamore and Groarty Road, but the Brits came behind us and closed them again before we eventually succeeded. Big McDaid would be there with his bulldozer and with help from Damien and Paddy Doherty, Philip McGilloway, Duck and about thirty others, they made short work of reopening the road at Lenamore a few times.

We also had been attempting to open the border roads for years before the ceasefires. One Saturday morning in the late 1980s, we sent a few people out ahead of us with their dogs to quietly check the area for any Brits or RUC lying in wait. They came back to tell us it was all clear. We ventured out, with the Donegal Comrades on the other side of the road and McDaid and his trusty Bulldozer being led by Eddie Fullerton.

As we started to open the road, what looked like a hundred Brits and RUC men emerged from nowhere and surrounded us all before arresting Eddie and about twenty others. So much for us scoping out the area intelligence-wise beforehand! Poor Eddie was held in a Strand Road police cell until that Monday, when we were all ordered up to Bishop Street Courthouse to account for ourselves!

Local council elections were due to take place in 1997, as was Westminster elections. Because of all the work I'd been doing locally on behalf of Gearóid Ó hEára, I was asked to run as a candidate that year alongside Gearóid in hopes of taking a seat from the SDLP and securing a second seat for Sinn Féin on the council. We also ran a third candidate, Bernadette McDaid.

* * *

I decided to run for Derry City Council in 1997. We set up our own Election Committee and Neil McLaughlin was made the Director of Elections. Neil had been a friend of mine for years, a steadfast republican but a very good amateur and professional boxer too. He had represented Ireland in boxing at the 1972 Munich Olympics Games before turning professional in 1976. One of Neil's fights in the Templemore Sports Complex descended into absolute chaos after British soldiers arrived and entered the fight arena itself, causing many an outburst or angry scene amongst the crowd there. It took a while to get the Brits out again, but after that it seemed to calm down and order was restored.

In May, just before the 1997 elections, all the North's election candidates were invited to a meeting in Monaghan to discuss plans for the coming days. It was a particularly long meeting that lasted all day, so I only got home to Derry at around 8pm that evening, and I headed straight for bed, exhausted after such a tiring day.

At about 3am, I was awakened by a knock at the door and when I looked out, I recognised a taxi-driver I knew – and he quickly told me there had been an explosion at the Sinn Féin centre and the centre was now on fire. I got dressed as fast as I could and headed up towards the office.

When I got there, the front door was blown off and the porch blown in. I was met by both the Brits and the RUC asking if I was the key-holder of the office. I was then joined by Gearóid Ó hEára and Jim Breslin before others started to turn up. The fire brigade extinguished the fire, but the RUC wouldn't let myself or Gearóid enter the office afterwards, claiming it wasn't safe. It seemed safe enough for the Special Branch and the Brits to enter once the fire was put out.

We protested about the length of time they were inside afterwards, clearly suspecting that they'd be searching for something to incriminate the party. This went on for a few hours, but they found nothing and left at 10am. It looked to us that the army did more damage to the premises than the bomb did.

The Waterside UDA admitted responsibility for the explosion on that day's lunchtime news bulletin, claiming it was in retaliation for IRA attacks in the city. It happened early in the morning, so nobody was there. We had to fix the place up and that's how close they could come into your community if they wanted to. Luckily we had put special steel reinforcements on the windows and doors. Over the next few days, we got the office cleaned up enough to carry on with the election campaign.

We fought a good campaign that year, setting up the Election Committee with Neil in charge and Jim Breslin as my election agent. I took the second seat on the City Council, with Gearóid and I coming in with similar votes overall of over 1,200 each. Sadly, our third candidate, Bernadette McDaid, didn't make it.

Our celebrations lasted for days. It was the first time Sinn Féin took a seat from the SDLP in their stronghold area of Shantallow, so it was worth celebrating. We had another two councillors elected too, Peter Anderson and Lynn Fleming, bringing our total number of elected councillors to eight on the Council. We were excited, it felt like Sinn Féin was on the move and progressing.

My election success was down to the hard work of our activists and supporters and the campaign waged by people like Terry Francis, Robbie, Alex, John, Fitzie and all our comrades in the Greater Shantallow area. Together, these men made their mark and helped us achieve what we did.

1. Shantallow councillor (later Derry Mayor) Gerry Ó hEára, on right, at the launch of the plans for the Northside Complex.
2. Tony to the left of the picture, chairing the ceremonies at the funeral of Eamon 'Bronco' Bradley. Also included are John O'Hagan (trumpet), Sean Keenan, Barney McFadden and Neil McLaughlin.
3. Shantallow residents at the launch of the plans for the new Village.
4. Tony taking part in what would become known as the original Bloody Sunday march in January 1972.

1. The newly-elected councillor for Shantallow is congratulated by party leader Martin McGuinness at the Guildhall in 1997.

2. Shantallow republican Alec O'Donnell taking part in a protest at Waterloo Place in the late 1970s, to highlight the conditions in the jails.

3. In his election suit, William Street, 1997.

4. Tony delivering an oration at the Republican Plot, Derry City Cemetery, in the 1980s

Republican leader Hugh McAteer speaking at a rally in Derry, flanked by Tommy Mellon, Seán Keenan among others.

Recently-arrived British troops searching vehicles on Craigavon Bridge in the late 1960s.

An Easter march in the 1980s.

Joe McCallion in the foreground at Derry Hunger Striker Patsy O'Hara's funeral.

Relatives Action Committee supporters protesting the conditions in the H Blocks at Free Derry Corner in the early 1980s. Veteran republican Barney McFadden is to the right of the picture.

On Guildhall Square, protesting the courts' use of 'supergrasses' in the 1980s. Included are Barney McFadden, Mitchel McLaughlin, Assemblyman Martin McGuinness and Tony Hassan.

Martin McGuinness, recently elected member of the short-lived 1982 NI Assembly, pictured at Fergleen Park after Tony asked him to inspect flood damage to fields in the area.

Republicans returning from a Derry civic parade in the late 1970s, during which they had stripped off the walls of their original float, an Irish country cottage, to reveal the bars of a H Block cell.

Tony and fellow councillor Marion Hutcheon are introduced to Senator Edward Kennedy by John Hume.

A Sinn Fein team from the early 2000s, includes Cathal Crumley, Mary Lou McLaughlin, Mary Nelis, Mitchel McLaughlin, Barney McFadden, Marion Hutcheon, Lynn Fleming, Peter Anderson and Tony.

Helping out at the candy-floss stall at the Earhart Festival.

The Shantallow team for the 2001 council elections. Included are Ollie Green, Jean McGinty, Tony, Ricky Halpenny, Peter McDonald and Gerry Ó hEára.

115

The Sinn Féin Derry City Council team promoting a 'Save the Peace Process Rally' in the early 2000s.

At the 2011 launch of the Bradley/Heaney Cup. Included are: Lynn Bradley (Bronco's sister), Martin McGilloway, Ciara Ferguson, TH, Peter 'Duck' McDonald and Eilis Heaney.

Inspecting the troops before the 2016 Centenary commemorations.

Pictured in 2013 with Mayor Martin Reilly and fellow councillors at a Freedom of the City reception for Foyle Hospice founder Tom McGinley.

The Shantallow office as it is today, with Ciara Ferguson MLA, Sandra Duffy, John McGowan and Pat Murphy.

Friends at Shantallow House, including the late Eamonn 'Lefty' Kelly and Martin Plunkett McGilloway.

The late Bobby Kelly (r) and Martin McGilloway (l) presenting John McCool with a trophy in memory of his father, John, who was a well-known quizmaster in Shantallow.

A meeting at Ráth Mór to discuss the crisis at Stormont in the months before Sinn Féin brought down the assembly (January 2017). Included are TH, Sean McMonagle, Martin & Bernie McGuinness, Pat Murphy, Sean McCloskey, A.D. Toland, Daisy Mules and Christine McLaughlin.

'Gills',Tony and Peter Anderson at a Bradley/Heaney Cup launch.

A lasting achievement for Councillor Hassan

At a function in the Gasyard Centre, following an anniversary mass for Kathleen Thompson, the Creggan mother of ten shot dead outside her home by a British soldier in 1971. Included are Martin McGuinness, Gerry Duddy and Bernie McDaid.

1. Grim faced, after the announcement that Sinn Féin will be barred from all-party talks in the late-1990s. Included are Mitchel McLaughlin, Barney O'Hagan, Martin McGuinness, Tony Hassan and Raymond McCartney.
2. Tony with his long-time friend John Doherty

The Shantallow Council team, featuring Sandra Duffy (later Mayor), Tony Hassan and Elisha McCallion (later MP).

Shantallow republicans at an anti-Brexit rally on the border at Killea. Included are Martin McGilloway, Gerry McLaughlin, Peter McDonald, John Gallagher, Tony Hassan and Paul Deehan.

Derry Sinn Féin representatives pictured in 2000 after the appointment of the city's first Sinn Féin mayor in almost a century. Included are Gerry Ó hEára, Barney McFadden, Gerry Mac Lochlainn, Tony Hassan, Cathal Crumley, Marion Hutcheon, Lynn Fleming, Peter Anderson and Mary Nelis.

At a dinner in the Tower Hotel marking the 25th anniversary of the Bronco Bradley cup. Included are Martina Anderson & Paul Kavanagh, Rose & Raymond McCartney, Mitchel McLaughlin, TH, Lynn Fleming and Patricia Logue.

When first announced, the development at Skeoge was going to be the biggest build in Ireland since Adamstown in County Dublin.

Inspecting the new housing development at Racecourse Drive.

After the fencing along the river at Culmore Village was damaged by vehicles, Tony Hassan led a campaign on behalf of residents to get a shorefront wall erected.

Tony outside Shantallow House. His friend Eamon 'Bronco' Bradley was shot dead by British soldiers as he was leaving the pub. Tony would chair the graveside ceremonies.

Admiring the first houses built as part of the Skeoge development, at Glenabbey.

Tony's grandson Callum Hassan who captained Derry City U-18s to victory at the Foyle Cup, pictured with parents Ciarán and Maureen.

1. Plans for the new social housing development at Springtown, currently being considered.
2. Outside the old Shantallow Community Centre.
3. With Emmerdale star Lucy Pargeter (Chas Dingle on the soap), during her visit to the Earhart Festival in 2007.

Shantallow republicans taking part in the Easter 2016 centenary commemoration events. Included are Martin McGilloway, Michael Gallagher, Liam Griffin, Stephen Fitzpatrick, Whitey Wilson and James Jennings.

The Guard of Honour at Shantallow republican Oliver McFadden's funeral. Included are Majella Cavanagh, Damien Doherty, Elisha McCallion and Pat Murphy. Tony gave the oration at the funeral.

At Madamsbank, calling for new safety initiatives at the roundabout. Traffic lights and new streaming systems were subsequently introduced.

Shantallow republicans pictured before the Easter 2016 commemorations. Included are former MLA, and hunger striker, Raymond McCartney, and Sandra Duffy, later Mayor of Derry.

Tony Hassan standing beside the welcome sign at the entrance to Shantallow.

Martin McGuinness makes a presentation on behalf of Shantallow republicans to Eilis Heaney, mother of IRA Volunteer Denis Heaney, in 2008.

1. Tony pictured with Martin McGuinness affixing the tricolour to his good friend Neil McLaughlin's coffin in 2013. The Shantallow republican, 65, had been an Olympic boxer, competing at the Munich Games. Also included in the photograph are: Gerry McCartney, Raymond McCartney, Martin McGilloway and members of the McLaughlin family.

2. The memorial stone at the Republican Monument.

CHAPTER 14
THE GOOD FRIDAY AGREEMENT AND GARVAGHY ROAD

The Good Friday Agreement was signed on April 10, 1998 by British prime minister Tony Blair and Irish Taoiseach Bertie Ahern and a referendum was held in both the North and South.

The agreement was approved by voters across the island of Ireland in the referendum held on May 22, 1998. Overall, the agreement was approved by 94% of voters in the south and 71% in the North - results that allowed for an assembly and power-sharing government to be set up in the north of Ireland. This new Assembly would include all political parties collectively for the first time in the North's history.

The assembly elections took place on June 25, 1998 with its first official sitting on July 1, 1998. Sinn Féin won eighteen seats in the new assembly, with Mitchel McLaughlin and Martin McGuinness elected for Derry.

Despite holding eighteen seats in the assembly, Sinn Féin were excluded from all-party talks in February 1998 due to alleged IRA involvement in two deaths earlier that month. Because of the refusal to let Sinn Féin into talks we held protests all over the place, including one big march that came from all directions in the city into one central point. We marched from Shantallow to meet the Ballymagroarty comrades and together we all marched to the town centre. That day there must have been over 20,000 people in the rally to support all-party talks. After lengthy negotiations, Sinn Féin entered the talks process that August.

That summer of 1998 saw a repeat of clashes and violence in Portadown as the annual Drumcree protests returned. For years, the Orange Order had been allowed to march down the Garvaghy Road against the wishes of the people who lived there. Basically, the people in Garvaghy Road were being held to ransom by the RUC and Orange Order. Every year, this caused protests and riots that rippled out beyond the Garvaghy Road and into most of the nationalist areas in the North.

In 1998, a new Public Processions Act led to the setting up of a Parades Commission to address parading issues. The Parades Commission then banned the Orange Order march from parading up the Garvaghy Road, which caused outrage in the unionist community. Residents were now locked in the area, surrounded by the RUC, British army and angry loyalists, but they still refused to let the Orangemen march down the road.

Residents needed help and support, and so different areas in the North organised relief cavalcades to Garvaghy Road to take them food supplies.

I travelled up with our convoy. We had organised fifteen cars and loaded them up with as much food as we could get. Local shops and businesses donated a lot of goods too, and it was really encouraging to see how much support we had. We set off at 10am, and Patricia Moore was with me in the lead car, followed by Peter McDonald, Dominic Doherty (who worked as press officer out of the Shantallow office before becoming Martin McGuinness's PRO), Ronnie Deehan, Dale Moore, Jim Breslin, Gurkie Gallagher and others.

When we arrived at the Garvaghy Road around dinnertime that evening, the whole area was filled with army and tanks and guns and it felt like a really heavy, really intimidating atmosphere.

Historically, security forces had locked down the Catholic area every year to allow the Orange parade through but the residents demanded change and succeeded in getting the march stopped. This led to the standoff at Drumcree between the security forces and thousands of Orangemen. It was a tense sight, but the ban was upheld despite days of violent disturbance, and the march is still banned from that route today.

We still had our own problems in some parts of Derry with rioting during election time. The problem was that there were cops in every polling station interfering with people coming in or out, which they had no authority to do, and if you issued any protest there was the possibility you'd be arrested.

After every election, our leadership took it up with the electoral authorities that police were not needed. In a democratic world, there are no police needed taking over polling stations. Seeing four or five land rovers in a car park was part of the problem, it put people off coming to vote and it antagonised the local population. I've always believed that young people were enticed to riot by others within the community, though. Orchestrated at times to confront the cops and keep the tension going.

After negotiations, the police did leave the polling stations. That first year they weren't there but compromised that they would come when the polls closed to take the ballot papers away. The first couple of years of that also caused rioting, just by them being in the area. It came to pass then that the presiding officers of the polling stations themselves would take the ballot papers and boxes to a central point and there was no problem. That's how the situation was solved really, we took the problem out of their hands. While that worked in our areas, there were still occasions of rioting at some stations in Creggan and in Carnhill during the 1990s. The last time Slievemore School was used for polling, there were no police anywhere but there was rioting and there was a bomb scare, which again put people off from coming out. We'd like to have Slievemore open again or another place in Galliagh because more centres available means more people will be inclined to come out to vote. It's an ongoing battle and the police are the biggest problem in that respect.

We didn't work with the police to sort it out - we worked with the electoral office and the government, and they worked with the cops. Once we accepted policing and were on the policing board, we could get more involved in debating and helping solve issues like this one.

* * *

For the next few months, I continued to find my way in the local council and get to know my constituents. Together, Gearóid and I sat to plan how we could best support and help the people in the Greater Shantallow area, and we decided on several issues to focus on. I was given council duty roles that included environmental services, planning, road service, housing and utilities, like sorting out local footpaths, roads and street lights, etc.

Derry's housing situation was historically bad with hundreds on the waiting lists for homes. I was appointed the party's Housing and Planning spokesperson for the city and hoped to resolve some of these housing problems.

My first experience in this role was a planning application submitted for 288 social homes at Cornshell Fields near Shantallow. Its developer, Paddy McGinnis of the Braidwater group, was having problems with the planners and came to me and Gearóid Ó hEára for help.

We organised meetings with the planning service to see if there was any movement on the application. We were told that the SDLP had problems with the development crossing the Old Racecourse track area on the land, but we persisted. After a few more meetings, we all agreed that due to the city's growing housing crisis the application should be approved.

Considering this was my first experience in housing matters as a councillor, it all worked out well and led to the creation of Cornshell Fields. The Fernabbey development came next, and between them almost 500 social homes were constructed by Braidwater. Encouraged by our work on Cornshell Fields, I realised that housing was a particular interest for me and decided to put all my energy into campaigning for more social homes in Derry. At that time, there was a real housing crisis in the city and almost 3,000 people registered as homeless on the waiting list for social homes.

Gearóid and I regularly met with the Housing Executive to see if more land could become available. There were enormous numbers of people coming to our constituency office looking for help getting a home. When the new builds became available, it was great to see young, one-parent families so happy at finally getting a new home of their own.

There were different elements to constituency work, including sorting out roads and street lighting problems for residents. There was also a lot of confidential work involved in the role, but this was naturally kept in-house.

As the 1990s drew to an end, Derry City Council began debating on how best to mark the millennium and various ideas were put forward. Eventually a decision was made to build a world-class theatre – the Millennium Forum Theatre and Conference Centre. We still had no site for this proposed theatre complex, and debates continued into potential sites in the city with little success.

At a full Council meeting in May 1998, council officers met us as we were going into the Guildhall and asked us to unite on ideas for the theatre site because the project's funders were inside at the meeting. Showing a united approach, we agreed to site the new theatre in the city centre near the East Wall.

In hindsight, however, I think we may have been too hasty in our decisions. It would have made far more sense to build the millennium project along the river at the Sainsbury's site, and for Sainsbury's to have opened up more centrally.

History was made in June 2000 when Cathal Crumley became the first Sinn Féin Mayor of Derry or any other Irish city since the early 1920s. As a former political prisoner and a blanket-man, Cathal had the backing of all the nationalist councillors on Derry City Council. That year I was given the role of chairperson of Environmental Services, and so if Cathal had too much on as mayor some of his duties would fall to me. He had an excellent year in office, and his wife Mary was an excellent mayoress of the city.

I sometimes think that we're fortunate to exist at this time and during such an historic period in Ireland over the past half-century. I'd love to know what people will say about this time in our history 100 years from now.

I've always felt that history has a habit of repeating itself in Ireland. Even within the last hundred years, we have had Bloody Sunday in Dublin in 1920 and Bloody Sunday in Derry in 1972; the War of Independence in 1916-1921 and the armed struggle of the 1970s-1990s and the signing of the Anglo-Irish Treaty in 1921 and the Good Friday Agreement in 1998. Let us hope that there are fewer repeats in the next hundred years.

CHAPTER 15
Securing the Skeoge and new homes

By now, Mitchel McLaughlin was an assembly man – that is, an elected member of the new Northern Ireland Assembly – which meant someone had to be co-opted on the local council in his place and so Gerry McLaughlin replaced him. Gerry was an ex-prisoner and, at one time, had been a spokesperson for Sinn Féin in England. He was an ideal candidate and a fantastic councillor for the city, capable of debating with anyone, no matter the subject.

When the next local government election took place in May 2000, Gearóid Ó hEára and I ran again, only this time the party had four candidates with Ollie Green and Jean McGinty nominated as our running mates for the area.

Gearóid and I were elected again, and another two Sinn Féin councillors were also elected, Paul Fleming and Billy Page. This meant the party now had ten councillors on Derry City Council and was continuing to grow. Look out, SDLP! With ten councillors, Sinn Féin had more powers within the council, too.

Many years earlier, in the 1980s or so, a new road was proposed to connect parts of the city although there had been no movement on it. Some residents from the Fernabbey area came to my office on Racecourse Road to reignite the issue of the proposed Skeoge Road development, which it had been called by then. At that time, the road itself ended at Fernabbey in a cul-de-sac, so the development was desperately needed to connect these areas to Buncrana road and open that area for Housing.

Most importantly, the Skeoge area was also zoned for housing which would give us the land we badly needed for more social homes. The official line from the Road Service was that the Skeoge Link is a road which will complete a route from the Foyle Bridge to Buncrana Road to Donegal. Councillor William O'Connell had lobbied for it for years before I came into council, and it was still a big issue. My view was this new road could open that whole area of land to further development. I knew that once we built the Skeoge Road, then that land would be opened up for housing. It was a battle because the planning authorities dragged their feet a lot. There was no more land around our areas to build but there was plenty of land at Skeoge and it made sense.

After meeting with residents, I got in touch with Mary Nelis who was an MLA for the city at that time for her help arranging a meeting with the Road Service and the Roads Minister at Stormont. In this meeting about a month later, we were told that the Road Service was anxious to progress the Skeoge, but that progress was being held up by the landowners themselves. That was the hardest part of my role on the project – trying to track down and working with the landowners for the new road. Even tracking them down or getting in contact was a nightmare for me, but I was determined to drive this project forward as much as I could.

I then brought it up at the council's planning meeting and asked planners to arrange a meeting between landowners and council, which took a while to sort out, but we did meet a few months later.

The landowners were based all over the place, so it was a huge juggling act to bring them all together. Some owners wanted to do a deal right away, but one owner refused to agree, and the meeting ended without an agreement. This went on for almost a year.

Another meeting took place with me, Raymond McCartney and Connor Murphy who was Roads Minister at the time, and the landowners. It must have lasted two hours but was worth it when everyone agreed a deal to get the project started.

Planning permission was granted in May 2006 and construction started in 2007 at a cost of over £5 million. The Skeoge Road was officially opened by Connor Murphy in 2008 and stretches 1.9km or 1.2miles, transforming the area. The late Willie O'Connell attended the opening with me and other councillors.

Now the Skeoge Road was open and operational, developments could begin, and I explored the opportunities of building social homes as there was plenty of land at Skeoge and lots of possibilities.

Fold Housing Association were the first such association to put in a planning application for 42 homes at Skeoge, and as usual, planners were taking their time. The manager of Fold came to me for help to get the application approved, so I met with planners who came up with a list of things Fold had to do first before getting approval. It was so frustrating, and I pointed out to planners that there were over 3,500 people currently on waiting lists and, considering the Skeoge was open and already zoned for housing – insisted the application should be approved.

Thankfully, a compromise was reached, and the planners allowed the first phase of 25 homes to begin. Within a month, they approved the other 42 homes too. It was this initial success in social housing that kick-started the massive building programme that has transformed today's Skeoge. I knew that if I got the first phase through, the rest would follow.

As Fold Housing Association was a leading association in the North, news of this first phase of homes was a good news story for others on the waiting lists.

I held more meetings with Fold to ask about further plans, and they were hopeful more homes would follow as they were in partnership with the Braidwater building group, who were building more social homes in the Glenabbey area for Fold. Following discussions with Fold and Braidwater, they shared that they wanted to build another few phases which, in total, could create as many as 300 social housing homes over two years. Again, this was fantastic news for all those still waiting for housing in the city.

The whole scheme at Glenabbey ended up with 380 social homes and a great big children's play park for the entire community to use. Fold later changed their name to Radius Housing Association.

Meanwhile, another group, Apex Housing Association, secured land in Skeoge for an initial first phase of 59 homes to be built on the site, but unfortunately, Apex encountered the same problems with city planners as Fold previously. It took several meetings and a great deal of patience before the Planning Service approved the 59 homes for Apex.

After these initial complications, the Planning Service themselves seemed to adapt and became quicker at approving applications – hence the many new estates and streets that bring life and community to the Skeoge Road today.

When the Skeoge area is eventually finished, Apex will have built many more homes there and, altogether, there will be in the region of 1,500 social homes there. At the lower end of Skeoge, Braidwater have another 300 private homes already in the pipeline.

I'm really proud of what I achieved in terms of the Skeoge Road development. For years, it was a major part of my council work and even the local newspapers associated me with Skeoge because at times I was always on the phone to them and trying to publicise the idea somehow.

The building of social homes in Skeoge is finished, but there is private housing still being built and planned on the green area between Lynch's supermarket and the last roundabout on Skeoge, as part of a new policy with planners is to build social houses along side private homes.

I feel there's a great possibility that this green area in lower Skeoge will eventually be given over. For social homes, we are badly in need of youth facilities and community services. Galliagh is only now getting the community services they deserve after thirty-five years – we don't want the same happening in Skeoge and it is beginning to look the same. Hopefully a youth facility and community centre with a 3G or 4G pitch might be built yet on the waste ground there, and land opposite that could be used for more housing.

I'm really proud of the role I played within local housing and some of the things I was responsible for during those years. I loved the possibilities – I didn't want a thank you or a bunch of flowers. I accepted the housing and planning role because I wanted to help with those issues in particular and to help people get homes I now realise - that all the hard work and perseverance was worth it. Helping families find homes of their own and helped our city expand where it mattered most.

CHAPTER 16
Community Initiative

For such a huge population that includes thousands of families with young children, the Greater Shantallow area of Derry suffered greatly from a lack of community resources and infrastructure.

In the mid-1990s, there were very few community or tenant groups operating in the area to support its residents. The Derry Resource Centre in Carnhill was the only community group available to help and advise people, but its services were limited, and many residents felt it wasn't doing enough to help residents of all ages living in Shantallow. As a direct result, several local people held a meeting in the community hall to which local councillors were invited – with the aim of establishing a new organisation that could help the community.

A new group was formed, the Shantallow Community Residents Association, and Cathal McCauley was voted in as its new chairperson. Similarly, another group was set up in nearby Galliagh, the Galliagh Development Group, and Brian Doherty was elected leader and Annette Nicholl (Doherty) the group's Secretary. Annette and her team knocked every door in Galliagh to see what people most needed in their community. She was a great worker and much admired by her colleagues and the community.

Leafair Community Association was also set up by residents in the early 1990s during a NI Housing Executive refurbishment scheme at Leafair Park. Its residents set up the group so they could collectively work with NIHE to support residents during the decant of their homes. Meeting in each other's homes, they planned a new vision for the area with better community infrastructure and community services for all. Importantly, all of these new community groups consulted with the wider community in their prospective areas through a residents/household survey that asked residents what they needed and wanted to see in their area.

The survey results highlighted the main issues of concern for residents in every estate, with one of the main areas for improvement being more play facilities for younger children, including play parks and football pitches. The survey also helped with the establishing of a range of health and wellbeing programmes for residents of all ages that would improve everyone's quality of life.

Alongside these new community groups were a number of women's groups set up, including Galliagh Women's Group with Rosie Doherty and Marie Gillespie doing some brilliant work in the greater Galliagh area. The Leafair Women's Group had Julie McDonald and Ann Gallagher at its helm, Shantallow Women's Group had Stella Cauley and, of course, Jean Cook's women's group in Carnhill all collectively supporting and empowering their own communities.

Originally based in Galliagh Park, the Greater Shantallow Community Arts organisation and its later addition, Studio 2, are an amazing resource set up by community worker Ollie Green. As creative arts hubs, both organisations have had a huge impact on people of all ages, not just in our area but across the North West too. Ollie has done a brilliant job bringing arts into communities and deserves so much credit for what he's achieved through the work of Greater Shantallow Community Arts, bringing people together creatively, particularly young people, and providing an outlet to express themselves.

* * *

In 1995, following a public meeting, chaired by Joe Martin, in St Brigid's College, a new organisation called the Greater Shantallow Area Partnership (GSAP) was formed to operate across all local areas. The idea of the partnership was to work collaboratively among residents, community and voluntary sector groups, Derry City Council and statutory/private organisations to help improve life for people living there. Since then, GSAP has been an invaluable resource for the entire area in terms of social, community, economic and physical regeneration. As a community support agency, the partnership's scope includes supporting a vast area of the city's outskirts - Galliagh, Shantallow, Carnhill, Culmore, Skeoge, Pennyburn and Ballynashallog.

GSAP's founding board, supported by the North West Development Office, consisted of twenty voluntary members including councillors and representatives from community/voluntary groups, residents, community businesses and from NI Housing Executive. The board developed a razor-sharp focus on what needed to be done and their vision was gradually delivered by Darren Kirby, the original community coordinator, assisted by dedicated staff and volunteers.

One of the first priorities of the Area Partnership was to carry out a wide-reaching community consultation and audit of the needs of residents in the Greater Shantallow area. This audit research resulted in GSAP publishing their August 1996 report, 'Building Successful Communities'.

From its early stages, the Area Partnership moved to its current base at

Northside Village Centre in 2002, with a further expansion of our premises in 2012 under the current chairperson Peter McDonald. As the partnership continued to grow, Peter McDonald led the successful delivery of a range of new community-led social, educational and employment programmes to help people, as well as capital investment projects and area-wide environmental and community events. I've no doubt that GSAP's vision and support has helped transform the Greater Shantallow area to what it is today, and that the training and opportunities it gave people has helped change a lot of lives.

GSAP's capital achievements over the years include creating an extension to the Rainbow Child and Family Centre and Galliagh Play Park, building Leafair 3G pitch, the Outdoor Gym and Men's Cabin, Shantallow Crazy Golf, MUGA and the football pitch. Their work has also enabled St Brigid's Parish Centre refurbishment, the building of a Family Room in St Paul's Primary School, the completion of Na Magha Hurling Club's new club house and the refurbishment of St Joseph's Boxing Club, to name but a few.

As there were ongoing problems with policing in Shantallow and other areas, the CRJ (Community Restorative Justice) was set up and led by Martin Connolly to support residents in identifying and addressing contentious issues in their areas and exploring options to resolve them.

Ciara Ferguson was the Partnership's rock and led the organisation with skill and was always a person that people found most approachable, and she really cared about the community itself and getting things done. She was continuously on the go, responding to the needs of residents and local neighbourhoods. In her time at GSAP, Ciara led on a range of best-practice projects such as the Extended Schools Cluster initiatives, the Family Support Hub and a series of programmes on Early Intervention, Employment Support and Youth Leadership. Each project that was developed in the Greater Shantallow Area, Ciara was somewhere behind it. Now she is an MLA for Foyle and I have no doubt she will perform well when the Assembly is up and running again

One project that I believe had a massive impact on people's health and wellbeing locally was getting the green-light to build Leafair's brand new lit-up 3G football pitch, which opened in 2011. The idea originated a few years earlier when Leafair Community Association urgently needed help building a fence around its football pitch. Neglected and unsecured, the pitch attracted a lot of antisocial behaviour, with joyriders setting cars alight on the pitch tarmac, damaging it further, and causing serious problems for the community.

I approached the Council about funding a fence to secure the pitch, but I was refused as it would cost too much. We then put our heads together to think of other ways we could upgrade the total area with a 3G pitch. Peter called a meeting and invited all the elected councillors, council officers, departmental officials from the-then Department for Social Development and someone representing the Area Partnership.

At the time, we were told that a 3G pitch with all the fittings, plus lighting, would cost in the region of £650,000 to build. It was agreed that if Leafair Community Association and the Area Partnership could secure at least half of the funding, then Derry City Council could potentially make up the difference, but only if the project was supported by all councillors at a full council meeting.

Almost a year went by and a cocktail of funding totalling over £300k in grants was secured by Peter and the Partnership. It was then up to Council to find the match funding, so we could only hope. In a joint proposal by myself and Colum Eastwood, we gained the support of the rest of the Council and subsequently, they secured the planning permission needed to complete the project.

I have to say, when Colum Eastwood came into Council as an SDLP Councillor, he worked well with all the groups in the area and with us, as did Brian Tierney and Angela Dobbins. This didn't happen in the past, in my experience, so it was a welcome change. As I've always said, we must work together if we want to deliver for the people who elect us.

Around this time, Northside Development Trust mooted the idea of developing a sports facility at the waste ground beyond Bradley's Pass, but because of the 3G pitch agreed for nearby Leafair, Northside wouldn't have been able to get funding for the same type of project so close by. Just like the Leafair land, this other site was fast becoming an eyesore with people dumping waste and cars burned. Joe McLaughlin from Northside Development Trust contacted me to get some advice on what could be developed on the site as something needed to be done. We talked about different things that the area still needed and, as Housing spokesperson, I suggested the potential of selling the land to a Housing Association for building social homes. New housing was still badly needed to address the housing waiting list, so it seemed like the obvious choice. Joe asked me to set up a meeting with the Housing Executive, who then agreed that there was a need for more social rented homes in the area.

Apex Housing Association were then contacted, and they expressed a keen interest in buying the land to build more social homes, which was fantastic news. Northside Development Trust sold the land to Apex, and they applied for planning permission and were approved. Apex went on to build a number of social homes at Racecourse Drive, and it turned out to be an excellent development.

Another project that stands out was when the parish priest of Steelstown Chapel asked to meet me about selling the Marian Hall Site, which by then was a run-down community centre. He felt strongly that Shantallow needed more bungalows for older people who were living in three-bedroom family houses. He found that many older resident's children had married and left home, so they wanted to downsize thus freeing up three-bedroom houses for new young families.

Again, Apex Housing Association were interested, but they weren't allowed to build bungalows due to Department of Social Development (DSD) regulations only allowing bungalows to be built to meet special needs demands, as agreed by an occupational therapist. This was a real shame and unnecessarily strict considering how many others would benefit from bungalow living. When they couldn't build bungalows, Apex proceeded to build 25 new social homes.

We've argued with the DSD for years about the growing need for bungalow type housing for our increasing older population their argument is that bungalows take up more land than building two or three storey apartments, but we also have enormous numbers of older people in our city just crying out for bungalows. I think older people are being denied their human rights for adequate housing, which is surely a necessity for an ageing population. Maybe it's time to seek a judicial review on the matter and have the courts decide what should be done.

CHAPTER 17
BUNCRANA ROAD AND THE H2 SITE

After Cathal Crumley, Derry's Sinn Féin mayoral streak continued with a strong election and two more Sinn Féin mayors from 2004 to 2006.

First was Gearóid Ó hEára, who was elected mayor in June 2004 with Joe Millar from the DUP as deputy mayor. Then in 2005, Waterside-based councillor Lynn Fleming took over the mayoral role. Lynn's brother, Volunteer William Fleming, had been killed on active service back in 1984.

Gearóid had a good mayoral year that included reaching out to the city's unionist community to foster connections. Lynn's year after that went well too, and during her term in office, Lynn held receptions in the Guildhall for the Volunteers families and also, at another time, for the Bloody Sunday families who were still waiting for the Bloody Sunday Inquiry to report back its findings. In 2009, Paul Fleming became mayor of the city, marking the first time that a brother and sister both held mayoral positions in the same council in the North.

I was present at a Derry City Council meeting in 2003 or 2004 when councillors were given a presentation on the proposed H2 Site at Buncrana Road, which sounded like an exciting project creating over 3,500 homes. We were told it would be the biggest housing development project anywhere in Ireland since the Adamstown development in Dublin, and that it could be as big as Strabane town. The plans included a school, retail services, community green spaces, play parks and some community infrastructure.

Three or more years later and frustrated by the lack of progress on the development the site's developers, Kevin Crumlish and McCormack Homes, came to us asking if Sinn Féin could weigh in and help get the project moving along. We arranged a meeting with the planners which was attended by me, my fellow councillor Billy Page, and Raymond McCartney MLA, but the planners remained non-committal and said the developers were to blame for delays. Several meetings later, there was still no movement on the H2 plans, so we took the problem to Stormont - but still got nowhere. The stalemate persists to this day.

Almost ten years later, there was still not a sod turned on the H2 site. By then it was 2012 and I made statement after statement to the local press and TV interviews on Channel 9 to highlight the H2 plans and try to force action. I spoke on BBC Radio Foyle's Mark Patterson Show too, and still the planning service did nothing. Finally, in 2014, over a decade after the idea was first presented to council, developers abandoned the project. I'm sure the whole debacle threatened to damage them financially, and enough was enough. I feel they were treated very badly by the planning service – and Derry lost out on a huge opportunity, (the H2 site is facing Barbers shopping complex on Buncrana road)

The local television channel at the time, Channel 9, was a great way for local councillors and the general public to connect with the broader community, and it gave people a platform to share local stories and to have their message broadcast to local audiences. Jimmy Cadden was the man to know at Channel 9 and was always really helpful and fair-minded in terms of what was broadcast. Sadly, our local television channel is no more, and it was terrible to see it end and close down. I'd still love to know the reasons behind its closure and why Channel 9 wasn't appreciated enough as an asset worth keeping and investing in. Another wasted opportunity.

Although the first attempt at developing Buncrana Road's H2 site didn't work out, its potential remained clear. And another attempt was made to develop the site. The Braidwater group later announced plans to invest £450 million in the site – hailing 'The Cashel' as hugely significant and one of the biggest housing projects in Europe.

Braidwater's managing director, Joe McGinnis, expects Phase 1 to provide as many as 250 jobs in the construction sector, boosting the economy and paving the way for substantial long-term development. Any time now, plans will get the green light and more families will have homes. It could be a catalyst for change in the North West, and an example to address its unacceptable levels of housing need. When the wider Buncrana Road upgrade happens – if it ever does - the H2 site will thrive as a new suburb of the city.

Braidwater finally got Phase 1 outline planning approval for 740 homes in late 2022, almost twenty years since the idea was first mooted to Derry City Councillors in the Guildhall. Things need to change - how long does it take for the planners to act? The H2 site isn't just valuable for housing, it could transform future road infrastructure in the city because of a certain road there.

If realised to its full potential, the Spine Road could someday link with the back of Creggan and, later, with a future third road bridge that could link up with the A6 and A5 to create a ring road around the city. We shouldn't hold our breath, though, as it's a long way down the road yet. In fact, I think Gearóid Ó hEára first mentioned it during his 2004-2005 year as mayor.

The Buncrana Road itself is another problem that could affect the overall H2 site as it's been earmarked for a widening upgrade for many years. As far back as 1971 when I first moved to Shantallow, houses facing St Patrick's Terrace on Buncrana road were vested by Road Service as they wanted to upgrade the whole A2 road through Derry to Donegal. When that early project fell through, Road Service sold the houses back to people to live in.

Plans emerged again in 2005, when the Road Service proposed upgrading Buncrana Road into four lanes. By now, Conor Murphy was an MP and responsible for roads. He was adamant to progress A2 plans and, for a while, we all believed the £50 million project would happen. Residents needed to be consulted and kept informed about the upgrade, so Billy Page, Raymond McCartney and I canvassed every house along the Collon and Buncrana Road area to talk to as many as we could. We spent time with residents and listening to their concerns about the upgrade and how it might affect them and their property.

Once again, the upgrade didn't happen. In the next assembly election Conor Murphy was replaced by a new roads minister, Danny Kennedy from the Ulster Unionist Party, and any upgrade plans went on the back burner. In December 2016, another new minister, Chris Hazzard, announced a package of funding to recommence the Buncrana Road scheme, but nothing happened. Except the costs of the upgrade had increased to £70 million.

On 8 May 2018, the Department for Infrastructure (DfI) Roads presented updated proposals to upgrade the A2 between Pennyburn Roundabout and the border with Donegal. The plans reinforced the A2's importance as a key link and main corridor from the city centre to County Donegal. There's no doubt that the A2 road improvement scheme will bring economic benefits and further regenerate the city and surrounding areas.

Derry is growing so fast in recent decades, it's vital we think ahead and future-plan to accommodate this growth. It's an issue that has compelled me throughout my political career and led to my interest in housing.

In April 2023, the Department for Infrastructure issued news that the scheme would be paused indefinitely while wider transport strategy plans were developed. By now, costs are estimated in the region of £85 million. Although the regeneration of prime sites like Fort George, the old British army barracks, isn't dependent on the A2 work, it could help create the momentum needed to regenerate and repurpose those key areas.

In another blow, the whole area's sewage system needs to be upgraded to the tune of £1.7 million from Coshquin pumping station all the way to the junction of Buncrana Road and Culmore Road. This is bound to impact on A2 plans.

Another lost opportunity was when the Arntz Belting Company site was approved for development and approval was withdrawn. Why? Why does it take so much longer to approve planning applications in Derry than in any other council area? I feel there's so much red tape involved in local planning, it's no wonder national and international companies are reluctant to invest here.

Ideally, there needs to be a debate and complete shake-up of the planning process to ensure it works for the region and not against it. Elected councillors can now demand accountability from the city's planning service, and change has been a long time coming – it's the least we deserve. Derry needs a planning service that's up to the job so we can fully realise our potential.

The old Thornhill College site in Culmore is another example of letting a prime site stagnate, and it's been nearly twenty years since Thornhill moved out. Plans for a retirement village on the riverfront site took more than six years to get approval. In my opinion, no developer should have to face so many hurdles getting projects over the line.

In 2021, Derry and Strabane Council's planning committee unanimously approved plans for the site which include a 57-bed care home and 53 semi-independent apartment units for over-55's, although no work has begun as yet. With the city bursting at the seams in terms of housing, we need more of these projects, not less. We need to work with people and not against them.

CHAPTER 18
The Assembly - Martin and Big Ian

I was re-elected again for Shantallow in 2005, but we lost Gearóid Ó hEára on votes, with Elisha McCallion replacing him on council. The concept of new super-councils was under discussion, and so at that time our four-year council terms were extended to six years in office.

During those years we all became more reliant on technology in our day-to-day duties. Derry was now an Electronic Council which meant council work was primarily conducted by email. Council also introduced laptops and mobile phones for all councillors and staff, and paperwork became paperless offices. Those of us unfamiliar with laptops were offered training. I hadn't a clue how computers work, but my friends and comrades, Bernie Heery and Sandra Duffy, were experts in comparison and showed me the ropes. Some of our local Cumann members helped me out too and I soon got to know how to work the computers.

In the weeks that followed, there was serious debate within our party about whether we should support the new set-up in policing. Both the Good Friday Agreement and the Patten Report recommended that the RUC be replaced by a new service, the Police Service North Ireland (PSNI). To us republicans, this was simply a name change and a new uniform. Would a new police force treat us any better? Compromise on this issue felt difficult. After numerous meetings, however, Sinn Féin decided to agree on policing and move on.

As is usual, any decision on policy must be discussed and ratified at the annual Sinn Féin Ard Fheis. I've been to many Ard Feiseanna, but that year's event was the biggest one I ever seen in terms of attendance, and the motion on the policing issue was passed.

I voted for the police reform, but it was a hard decision for me personally as I still saw the PSNI as an extension of the old RUC. Either way, change was long overdue and in the interest of peace, agreeing was the right thing to do. Compromise wasn't welcomed by everyone, though, and a small number of members resigned from the party after Sinn Féin voiced their support for policing reform. Difficult decisions were necessary to make peace work. Our leadership, Martin McGuinness, Gerry Adams and Michelle McLaughlin worked hard to keep the party united throughout this period of compromise and change.

Looking back, I feel that those years after the Good Friday Agreement were a time of immense change for Sinn Féin. Even during the most intense top-level negotiations on policing and other matters, our leaders kept the rank-and-file party members informed every step of the way.

Meanwhile, in Shantallow, the constituency office was inundated with people looking for housing at the new Skeoge development, which kept Sinn Féin councillors constantly busy. It was a few years into the Skeoge development and new build projects were transforming this new suburb.

The housing system worked on a points system, and 200 points were the necessary requirement to be allocated a house, depending on how many children you had and other factors. If you had 200-plus points for a house at Skeoge, you got one, but it was still hard to reach that level and many families had been on the waiting lists for years without reaching the 200 points needed to be allocated a home. We would try to get their points to a high enough level to increase their chances of housing.

Some of the more serious cases are hard to forget, and most were one-parent families in desperate need but stuck in limbo. We'd write letters on their behalf to help get them more points for allocation, and sometimes it worked and sometimes it didn't.

We were fortunate that Housing Executive staff at our Collon Terrace office were particularly helpful and sympathetic to those in need. During my time as an elected councillor in Shantallow, I've worked closely with several very understanding housing managers there, including Seamus Kelly, Walter Mullan, Kevin McDowell and Eddie Doherty, as well as its Chief Executive, the late Paddy McIntyre. Allocation officers like the late Paul Devine, Damien Moran, Jackie Nixon and others were a great help to people too, as were the maintenance officers Tommy Morrison and Willie Cregan.

I was so saddened to hear about the passing of Paul Devine from the Collon office in 2022. Paul was always so helpful to many young families in the city and really took the time to listen and help people find housing accommodation. His is a terrible loss for his family and the entire community that he helped so much. Thanks for everything, Paul. Rest in peace.

* * *

In summer 2003, a new Monument Committee was established to look into the possibility of upgrading the republican monument in Shantallow. As it was, the monument needed a lot of work to bring it up to a standard befitting the local Volunteers who gave their lives in the Shantallow area.

The new committee consisted of myself, Martin McGilloway (Gills), Peter McDonald, Damien Doherty, James McGilloway, Seamus Soal, Bobby Kelly, Boyler, Sean McGlinchey and Dominic O'Kane. After some thought, we decided to relocate the monument to another part of Shantallow entirely onto the green space at Drumleck Drive. This meant dismantling the old monument, but both the committee and the Sinn Féin Cumann of the area agreed it was worthwhile to do so. We then enlisted an artist to come up with a few designs for the new monument before deciding on the final option for Drumleck Drive.

Before any work could start, we needed funding. To raise money, we organised various raffles and sponsored walks. Boyler organised a team to climb Mount Errigal on a sponsored walk, which was a fantastic fundraiser. We also got a lot of donations towards the new monument, and in the end, we had enough funds to go ahead with the project.

We needed a special type of stone which could only be sourced in Galway of all places. Undaunted, Dominic O'Kane found himself a lorry, and he and Sean McGlinchey and Damien Doherty headed down to Galway quarry to pick up the stone and bring it back to Derry.

It took the committee about six to eight months to complete the project but when finished, it was a fitting tribute to our local heroes; Junior, Gerard, David, Michael, Jim, Dennis, Bronco and Tony. The new monument is also a testament to Damien Doherty, who worked so hard alongside the rest of us to make it happen and who died in 2018.

* * *

At Stormont, full power had devolved to the Northern Ireland Assembly since 1999 but was revoked on several occasions over the years. In October 2002, the Assembly was suspended when unionists abandoned power-sharing after Sinn Féin offices at Stormont were raided by the police.

In March 2002, an assembly election was called and Sinn Féin and the DUP became the largest parties in the Assembly, with Ian Paisley and Martin McGuinness becoming joint First Ministers.

Despite their titles, the roles of First Minister and Deputy First Minister were equal and had the same powers and responsibilities, so the power-sharing dynamic was dependent on their working successfully together. Martin himself proposed the titles be changed to the more accurate 'joint First Ministers' and he used that term himself on occasion, but it was never changed.

This government was the first to last the full term. During that period, Westminster transferred all powers on policing and justice back to the assembly.

Big Ian retired as First Minister in 2008, and the 2011 assembly election saw his predecessor Peter Robinson elected alongside Martin McGuinness to lead the assembly. When Peter Robinson took over from Big Ian, relations between him and Martin McGuinness were no doubt frosty at first, but both men worked hard to develop a good working relationship.

In 2010, Peter Robinson stood down as First Minister after his wife was embroiled in some controversy, and Arlene Foster replaced him in office. The previous DUP First Ministers, Paisley and Robinson, had developed good professional relationships with fellow leader, Martin McGuinness, but with Arlene Foster in the assembly, the cracks became immediately apparent. It was clear from her body language and attitude that she didn't share her predecessor's humility to power-share with Sinn Féin for the sake of peace. I doubt she ever developed that kind of respect for republicans in office.

In my opinion, the 2007 pairing of Ian Paisley and Martin McGuinness was the strongest of any within the assembly leadership. Grit and determination gave them a certain strength to lead together, and it worked despite their massive political differences. The assembly has lacked that strength since.

Membership of the party was increasing in our area and Seamus Soal was now the chairperson of Shantallow Sinn Féin. By this time, the new monument was close to completion, and we had to plan how we would officially dedicate it to the community's fallen Volunteers.

Seamus set up an organising group to plan the unveiling event. I was asked to chair proceedings, with Raymond McCartney delivering the oration and Martin (Gills) McGilloway reading the Republican Roll of Honour. The commemoration took place in the evening and went really well. A special commemorative dance was held after the ceremony with the families and friends of our dead Volunteers as honoured guests.

Creating the new republican monument was a joint achievement of a team of people behind the scenes, but a few stand out as going above and beyond to make it a reality. Dominic O'Kane, Damien Doherty and Peter McDonald were the backbone of the project, and Sean McGlinchey sourced all the concrete and tarmac we needed to finish everything off. They made us all proud.

* * *

As part of my housing work some year earlier, I was called out to the Travelling community's site in Ballyarnett to see the state of the so-called houses this community were forced to live in. The Housing Executive had taken over the running of the site from Derry City Council, which was just as well, in my opinion, as I felt Council could have done a lot more to help this particular community over the years. The families on the site were living in terrible conditions and were in desperate need for real housing and basic amenities.

I began meeting with the Housing Executive to explore the possibility of constructing new-build homes for families there. Negotiations were successful and the Housing Executive agreed to ask Apex Housing Association to construct twenty new homes in Labre Park, adjacent to the existing site, and plans for a community centre too. It took two years to finish building Labre Park - an estate exclusively for members of the Travelling community – including its new community centre. When ready in December 2008 it was officially opened by the-then President of Ireland, Mary McAleese, which was such a huge honour.

Labre Park is one of the projects I'm most proud of throughout my working career. The families in Ballyarnett needed someone to speak up on their behalf, and I'm just glad I was in a position to do so, and that we were able to make such a difference to the lives of the Travelling community there.

I was very touched to be selected as an honorary guest at the 2010 Annual Volunteers Dinner Dance in the Guildhall. With all my family there it was a privilege and honour I'll never forget, and what a night it was with over 300 people gathered for the dinner dance.

An 'honorary' is kept in the dark until the night of the dinner dance itself. Before then, decisions would be kept a very close secret. During the event all Cumainn in the city were to be presented with an award, and Seamus Soal, our Shantallow chair, tried to get me onto the stage to accept the award on their behalf. Naturally, I agreed – not knowing this was a ruse to get me on stage. Once on stage, they announced that I was due an honorary award, and I was presented with this award by Martin McGuinness, which meant a lot.

Martina Anderson read aloud a statement recognising me as the honorary guest that year, and she never left anything out in the wonderful tribute she paid to me. Seeing my family sitting there, smiling, it really was a night to remember.

CHAPTER 19
Super Council, Elections and Brexit

Plans were still underway for an overhaul of how local services were organised, and this included radically reducing the number of local councils in the North. For a few years before it was implemented, elected representatives were required to serve a longer term in office to allow time for the parties to deliver on the way forward.

There was a lot of debate within and between political parties on the best ways to deliver the new program of government at local level. In the end, an agreement was reached that eleven new 'super councils' would officially take over from the twenty-six old ones with increased authority over planning and local regeneration. Among the new council functions would be full powers on planning, leisure and community services and on building control, local economic and cultural development. It would be the biggest change to local government in decades, hence taking years to plan and develop.

I was delighted that local councils would have full powers on planning issues. In my view, this was one of the biggest problems in the old council system. At times, I've seen a full council of 30 members in the chamber vote against a planning application, and it made no difference, so it will be the first time that councillors will have a say on planning applications that come before council.

As the 2011 local government elections approached, the Electoral Office told us that this election term was only for three years as the Assembly had set a date for the new super councils. A shadow council would come into effect for one year before in 2014, so change was set for 2015.

Myself, Elisha McCallion and Sandra Duffy, who was standing for the first time, were selected to run in Shantallow and hoped to take the third seat for the party. When the campaign kicked off, my canvassing team came out in strength as usual and did their best as always. In all the elections I fought since 1997, my canvassers never let me down, like Alex O'Donnell, Jim Breslin, Bobby Kelly, Neil McLaughlin, Bobby Sheerin, John Doherty, Fitzie, Duck and Gills, Martin Connolly and all the others who worked so hard to get Derry candidates elected.

We put in a good campaign, and Elisha and I were elected but Sandra didn't make it through. She did get a great vote, though, and vowed to stay with team

Sinn Féin to build for the next election which would be an especially important one. From then, we had three years to build and prepare for the implementation of the super councils. It was agreed that Sandra would work alongside myself and Elisha to build her profile ahead of the next election, which she did.

Ahead of three of us running in the next elections, the area was split up into three working areas to focus on and I was allocated the Culmore area. While we did have some support in Culmore, we still needed more, and I was tasked with increasing our support there to try and secure the party a third council seat.

I needed to find out what was most needed in Culmore. Its residents had very little community infrastructure besides one football pitch and one play park at Ballynagard that was a mess. Calling a meeting with local representatives seemed like the best next move, and this meeting involved reps from the Culmore football team, the local parish priest and a number of elected representatives.

From this, it was agreed to form a community group, the Culmore Community Partnership, and further agreed that Neil Doherty would be chairperson of the new group. A list of five projects was drawn up, and some of my colleagues from Greater Shantallow Area Partnership, Ciara Ferguson and Darren Kirby, offered their expertise and the support of GSAP in helping the new partnership progress its projects and aims.

The priority projects were outlined as a 3G football pitch, play parks for children, the development of the Culmore Country Park to include a community centre, play facilities and sports pitches, and to develop the old Victoria Hall as a state-of-the-art community hub. I take great pride in knowing that I set the partnership up and helped to get things moving in Culmore.

Derry's year as City of Culture in 2013 was a great success and brought so many amazing events and opportunities to the city. Particular highlights of the culture year for me would be the Sons and Daughters concert at the purpose-built culture Venue in Ebrington and the Turner Prize being hosted from there also. The biggest and most significant event of the culture year was undoubtedly the all-Ireland Fleadh Cheoil being held here – its first time ever in the North – and the entire city centre coming to life with music and craic for it.

Over the next few years, social housing projects in Skeoge continued to grow to the extent that we were concerned that, so far, there had been no talk of adding the community infrastructure that these new residents would surely need. The community and residents of Skeoge didn't want to see another Galliagh, where homes were built but not the basic infrastructure to help these communities work.

Action was needed on the issue, and the Greater Shantallow Area Partnership set up a Skeoge Strategy Group bringing together local councillors, developers, representatives of Apex Housing, council officials and others to plan ahead. These new plans needed to urgently deliver some sort of community infrastructure to the Skeoge area to help the growing communities there.

Apex Housing at that time were constructing quite a large building in Skeoge, and so Ciara Ferguson from GSAP initiated discussions with Apex about leasing the building from them for a Community Hub of sorts. Apex agreed, and once building was complete, GSAP hired a Project Manager for the new hub to develop ideas to benefit the area.

Among the projects suggested by Skeoge residents were a community centre, a 3G football pitch, a major play park for children and youth facilities. The Strategy Committee set in motion plans to liaise with various bodies to see if this could be achieved, the first of which was a meeting with the Education Authority. This was very useful as there are two sites zoned for schools in the Skeoge lands.

Ciara Ferguson, Darren Kirby and Karen Mullan MLA had several meetings with the Education Authority, and it transpired that the EA might only need one of the Skeoge sites for a future school. Naturally, the strategy group aired the possibility of the second vacant site being used for youth facilities instead. If the EA agreed, GSAP could then convince them to buy the land from Braidwater – who themselves were very supportive of what GSAP were trying to do for Skeoge residents.

Despite the number of new homes being built at Skeoge and other parts of the city, the numbers on the housing waiting lists got bigger still. We still needed more housing development to meet Derry's growing needs. When the British government took away the right to build and borrow funds from the Housing Executive in the 1990s, they created a situation in which housing associations controlled much of the new-build development.

* * *

We were now approaching the 2014 Local Government Elections, which would be the election to the new super councils across the North.

For the first time, Ballyarnett District Area was a six-seater election having previously been five seats. Sandra, Elisha and I were nominated to run for the party again and we formed an election committee with Patricia Moore as Director of Elections. I had my old canvassing team in place alongside some Culmore supporters, Shaun Maguire taking the lead with Pat Murphy and James Jennings also playing a big part that worked well with the team of canvassers. We also had Gerry Dyer doing the tally for us.

The campaign went well, and I was re-elected for Ballyarnett alongside Sandra and Elisha. We took the third seat, and the SDLP got two seats, with an independent candidate taking the last. That first year we were a shadow council ahead of the 2015 shake-up. For the time being, the old Derry City Council conducted business as usual.

After years of planning and preparation, in April 2015 local councils across the North finally underwent a complete restructure with twenty-six local councils reduced to eleven super councils with increased local governance.

As a result, Derry City Council expanded to become Derry City and Strabane District Council, and now had increased powers to deal with services such as planning, local economic development, car parking and community investment.

The first mayor of this new supercharged Derry and Strabane District Council was Elisha McCallion, who spent a year in office from 2015-2016. Elisha was an excellent and welcoming mayor and did the city proud during her twelve months as its First Citizen.

Among the new council's first priorities was developing a new area plan for Derry/Strabane 2025-30 as the previous plan was no longer viable. Although this was due in the first term of the new council, it wasn't completed then nor in council's second term either.

At last, the council had expanded powers over planning issues, and the processes themselves were updated to give council more responsibility and sway in future planning decisions. It was an improvement from the older planning practices but not perfect.

In terms of elected representatives, I felt that conditions and wages could also be improved if the council required full-time councillors.

* * *

After years of campaigning by British Tory politicians, in 2016 we were thrust into a referendum we didn't want, to leave the European Union. The referendum took place on Thursday June 23 2016, and the north of Ireland voted to remain within the EU, as did Scotland, but England voted to leave and so leave we did. In the end, England's vote outweighed all our Remain votes and it was voted to leave the EU by 52 percent to 48 percent.

Brexit, as it has since been called, was enough of a problem for many, but here in the North it posed a greater problem as unionists overwhelmingly voted to leave. This would cause them untold problems later down the line when they perceived a new customs border as breaking their union with England.

This vote to leave the EU was followed by years of negotiations and wrangling between the British, the Irish government and the EU, over terms and plans for Brexit. After chaotic negotiations, the British left the European Union on 31 January 2020, and we were powerless to intervene. I think we've done a great disservice to our children and grandchildren by leaving Europe.

The decision to leave is already backfiring for unionists in the North. When Brexit kicked in, so did the new customs protocol safeguard the special customs situation of the North – because the south is still in the EU. Basically, the protocol meant additional customs checks on goods between here and England, but this so-called border in the Irish Sea now has unionists doing a U-Turn over Brexit's ripple effects. Some unionists claim this invisible goods border in the Irish Sea is the biggest change in the North since partition. How interesting that they claim this now, as unionists mark the centenary of the North's partition. They steadfastly refused to reinstate Stormont until this protocol issue is dealt with – but it's already a done-deal on all sides with no chance of changing it. Do we not have bigger problems than invisible borders and fights over frozen meat? Unionism's control over the North is waning at last, and everyone knows it.

* * *

Elisha was Mayor of the new Derry City and Strabane District Council, and while it was a learning process at first, the transition to a bigger council worked very well. I was a committee member on planning, and it felt great to now have a say in what was approved or planned. The bigger council also brought in some newer councillors from Strabane and other outlying towns and while this was a big change it was a positive one as we expanded and made new connections.

Time is hard on all of us, and we have lost many good friends and comrades in the years since Derry and Strabane's super-council began. Derry's republican community will never forget people like Neil McLaughlin, Alex O'Donnell, James McGilloway, Jim (Hitler) Breslin, Terry Frances, John Oakley and old John McCool.

I felt honoured to give the graveside oration of my dear comrades, Neil McLaughlin and Jim Breslin. They deserved no less. Neil and Jim were dedicated to the republican cause and will always be remembered as leading from the front. Like so many other republicans deeply opposed to internment and British rule in Ireland, when there was serious work to be done you could rely on Neil and Jim and were never found wanting.

Neil spent a lot of his life touring Ireland and promoting the political message of Sinn Féin. His home in Shantallow was always open to republicans, as was Jim's, and supporting political prisoners and their families was always top of their list. Regardless of how busy they might be, Neil or Jim always ensured that people on the run had a safe bed for the night.

Neither Neil or Jim ever shied away from their responsibilities to the movement and city, and it was dedication like theirs that made sure the republican struggle stayed strong at a time when many might have faltered. They played leading roles in the Hunger Strikes protests and later supported the peace process and the Good Friday Agreement and worked for Sinn Féin until they fell into bad health.

We also lost Jim's close friend, Volunteer Hugh Duffy, and Barney McFadden, John Doherty, Dale Moore, and Paddy Mullan. The effort and dedication that these republicans gave to the struggle was enormous, and each was buried with republican honours.

Well known by many as the communications man behind the party, Dale Moore was a gentleman and an active and admirable republican. His death was a loss not only to his family, but to the party itself and to his sister, our esteemed member Patricia Moore.

Just after the elder John McCool died in Shantallow, I remember his son, John, approached me about joining Sinn Féin to carry on his father's work. Of course, I was moved by this request because it was exactly the right thing to do, and young John carried on where his father left off, supporting the party To the present day.

* * *

Losing Martin McGuinness, was a tragedy we will never get over and I can't overestimate how important Martin was to his family and friends but also to Sinn Féin as Assembly leader and joint First Minister. We were all shocked at how sudden the illness took him. When Martin died on March 21, 2017, it was something none of us expected and it was devastating. To me, it felt like the entire city was in mourning. As were Ireland's republicans far and wide.

Martin gave everything in reaching out to unionism in all its hostility, getting very little in return. He risked everything but persevered. When future Irish history books are written, I'm sure Martin McGuinness will feature front and centre for his role in modern Ireland and in helping secure peace.

Martin's close friend and lifelong republican, Jamesy Quinn, passed away the following year, which I thought poignant in a way as Martin used to say he felt safe and secure with Jamesy by his side.

In the final months of his life, Martin McGuinness kept working until he could work no more. By then, the DUP were in serious hot water for their handling of a scandalous renewable energy heating scheme which saw unionist farmers heating empty barns and sheds just for funding. Despite numerous red flags and warnings, the DUP allowed this to snowball until the corruption was estimated to cost us taxpayers £490 million overall. Yet Arlene Foster still refused to accept the DUP's role in the mess and her attitude grew more hostile.

I really admire the fact that Martin McGuinness didn't go quietly and that his final act as joint First Minister was to resign in protest at the renewable heating scandal – leading to Stormont's collapse. Like many in the North, he'd had enough of the conduct and attitude of the DUP who still refused to accept responsibility for colossal failings.

Martin delivered a masterstroke in resigning, because stepping down meant Arlene Foster lost her first minister role too. Integrity was everything to Martin and rather than let that DUP charade go on, he chose one final act of noble defiance that brought down the assembly on his way out.

CHAPTER 20
The End Game

The death of Martin McGuinness hit the Derry community and wider republican community very hard. Power-sharing had collapsed in 2017 after Martin's departure, leaving the assembly suspended for three years after that. Despite Stormont powers being suspended, elected MLAs continued to support constituents and fulfil their roles as best they could without a functioning government.

Elisha McCallion was co-opted into the Assembly after Martin's death, leaving a place on Council that was then taken by Caoimhe McKnight. A few months later, the Westminster elections were due, and Elisha was nominated by members at the Republican Convention, to stand against Mark Durkan from the SDLP.

Elisha won her Westminster election in 2017, becoming the new Sinn Féin MP for Foyle and beating the SDLP for the first time. Historically if elected to parliament, Sinn Féin MPs abstained from taking their seat within Westminster. To do so requires swearing an oath of allegiance to the British monarch – something no republican will ever do. Elisha's new role left a seat in the assembly and so Karen Mullan was co-opted in to fill Elisha's seat and did some great work as an MLA.

Raymond McCartney retired from the NI Assembly in 2020 after a long, successful career in politics, first as political prisoner and hunger striker, then as local elected MLA. Raymond made his mark in history.

At this time in January 2020, Martina Anderson was no longer an MEP (Member of the European Parliament) and so she was co-opted into Raymond's vacant seat at Stormont and took over the role. All the while, the Assembly remained in limbo with little direction until power-sharing was reinstated in January 2021, three years after it fell.

Meanwhile, the new, expanded Derry City and Strabane District Council continued the public consultation on the new Derry/Strabane Area Plan. In addition, the planning service gave all Council areas the right to set up a local growth partnership to explore and address needs in each area. Martin Connelly was elected chairperson of the Shantallow group.

After thirty years of sustained campaigning for local facilities, Greater

Shantallow residents were thrilled to get the green light for a new £1.5 million state-of-the-art Galliagh Community Centre in October 2018. Plans for the new centre showed that it would be built in the heart of Galliagh, behind the old co-op and White Chapel, and that it would house community organisations like the Galliagh Women's Group, Community Youths, Galliagh Residents Association, Teach Na Fáilte, Community Restorative Justice, and the Rainbow Child & Family Centre. The finished centre was opened in December 2022.

Likewise, plans for a £1.2 million community pavilion were granted to the nearby Leafair Community Association in a deal to be delivered by them and Derry City and Strabane District Council with supporting funding from the Social Investment Fund (SIF).

(2019) The Leafair Wellbeing Village was officially opened in November 2019, offering both office and recreational space for the community and local sporting organisations as well as four new sports' changing rooms. The whole development was started by Peter McDonald, who always knew what the community needed most. The new Leafair building also held the Men's Health Workshop and the Good Morning Northwest programme, which is a wonderful one-to-one telephone service that befriends and supports our older, more isolated residents in the community.

It was good to see big planning applications progressing through the system and being approved faster than before. Processes had improved considerably since the council reshuffle, but I always felt there was still so much more to do. Maybe that's the real lesson of politics. We celebrate small successes in this and that, but in reality - we know we could have done more and achieved more.

In total, I served over twenty years as an elected representative on Derry City Council and later, on its expanded Derry City and Strabane District Council. In those two decades I've seen so many ups and downs and had some unforgettable life experiences, but I truly did enjoy my time representing and serving the people of Greater Shantallow, Galliagh and further afield.

As the first term of our bigger Derry/Strabane council ended, we elected representatives readied ourselves for more elections and canvassing. First a decision was needed on who would run in 2019. In some ways, this second term was even more important than its first, as the wider area plan was still not finalised, and council still had a mountain of work left to do.

It was around this time in 2018 that our Director of Elections approached me - on behalf of the Derry Comhairle Ceantair - to ask if I would consider standing down from council. I can't describe how shocked I was to hear this proposal. Quitting wasn't something I'd ever considered before - either personally or professionally

After half a century faithfully serving the party, and twenty years of that as an elected representative for the people, I presumed I'd be able to fulfil my duties and retire from council at my own behest - after achieving all I possibly could. I'd planned for another term in council until 2023. Over 3,500 people were still in housing stress and in a homeless situation. In the city these people need to be supported for accommodation and not let the city planners off the hook

For a time, I debated with the Comhairle about all this, but the decision had been made, and after a few months I stood down.

Sinn Féin now had a policy of bringing young people forward to lead, and while I support this policy, I wasn't ready to stand down and relinquish my political career, but because of some health problems I thought it was time to stand down.

In April 2020, just as Covid-19 took hold, I was diagnosed with prostate cancer. I've been having treatment, but to hear you have cancer takes a lot out of you. At this point I would commend all the doctors and nurses at the cancer clinic in the city and all at the Altnagelvin complex for the help care they give to our community. The government should hang their heads in shame for the way they have treated them, we all must support them in their fight for better conditions and wages.

Men, if you have any signs of prostate problems go to your doctor right away. In hindsight, I waited a bit too long before seeking advice, but hopefully got it in time.

The 2019 local election listed four candidates to run; Sandra Duffy, Caoimhe McKnight, Aileen Mellon and Neil McLaughlin, the son of my friend Neil, who had sadly passed away just a few years earlier.

At the Sinn Féin convention that same year, most members were against running four candidates because of unfavourable conditions at that time – but these protestations fell on deaf ears. On election day, the four Candidates fought a good Election but only two got elected, Sandra Duffy and Aileen Mellon.

We lost five Sinn Féin councillors that year in Derry City and Strabane District Council - and all because the leadership refused to listen to its grassroots members.

In all, we only returned eleven Sinn Féin councillors in 2018, the same number of council seats as the SDLP. On paper, however, we remained the largest party in council because we had more first preferences votes than any other party.

More bad news was on the way. In September 2019, Britain's desperate and shambolic new prime minister, Boris Johnson, called a snap election in Westminster after his no-deal Brexit plans were rejected.

Elisha McCallion was selected once again to run for Foyle, but this time Elisha lost her seat by 17,000 votes to Colum Eastwood from the SDLP. These were among the worst election results in Derry Sinn Féin's history - signalling a tense and uncertain time for the party in polls and in the communities.

* * *

During my time in council, I've seen six Town Clarks from the old system, and one impressive Chief Executive, John Kelpie, in the new council. I've welcomed numerous mayors, served under new party leaders, and I've met the president of Ireland and international states-people including Senator Edward Kennedy and former President Bill Clinton in his second visit to the city.

I presumed I'd seen and experienced a bit of everything in my lifetime - that is, until we were faced with a global pandemic for the first time – an event that paused the world as we knew it.

After warnings of the virus spreading, it was suddenly here in Ireland and the entire country shut down. In March 2020, we had to close the Sinn Féin office as the Covid-19 pandemic raged on – and besides a brief hiatus that September, the office remained shut until May 2021.

The pandemic took its toll on us all. When Covid-19 forced the closure of all our shops and facilities, the Greater Shantallow Area Partnership swung into action to organise and deliver hundreds of food parcels and vouchers to local homes. Ballyarnett District Area were equally as proactive in terms of supporting us and rolling out their own emergency plans for isolated families and older, more vulnerable residents.

Leading the charge as usual were people like Ciara Ferguson, Peter McDonald, Darren Kirby, Cathal McCauley and Rory McParland, although they're just a fraction of the people who went to where they were needed most. I feel indebted to them, as we all should be. They're a credit to this city.

Since then, I've been on the side-lines watching as politics moves on. In July 2021 there was another co-option in Shantallow as Aileen Mellon stood down from council after two years and Damien Mullan was co-opted in her place.

* * *

A review was needed to find out why we lost so many votes and it was carried out by senior republicans from Belfast. The Ard Comhairle of Sinn Féin, its national executive board, agreed to revisit the Derry review report and scrutinise its findings further. Sinn Féin President Mary Lou McDonald immediately called for another, more expansive review of the Derry situation and appointed top senior republicans from both Dublin and Belfast to carry it out.

The Dublin-led review took a few months to complete and report back. When it did, their findings suggested a new Comhairle Ceantair be formed in Derry. This was a good move, in my opinion, and a sure sign that the Ard Comhairle recognised some of the deeper problems within the party in Derry.

The recommendation of the Ard Comhairle review led to Sinn Féin MLAs, Martina Anderson, and Karen Mullan, standing down.

With the next Assembly election scheduled for May 2022, the party now needed to consider replacement candidates for Martina and Karen's seats. Party members in the city nominated four potential candidates: Amy Hamilton, Padraig Delargy, Tiarnan Heaney and Ciara Ferguson, and a convention then voted in favour of Padraig Delargy and Ciara Ferguson, and they were co-opted onto the NI Assembly in place of Karen and Martina.

Martina and Karen were both offered positions within the party, which I was delighted to see as that wasn't always the case for others who stood down from office and weren't offered anything else. In hindsight, I'm sure there must be ways to handle problems within Sinn Féin. After all, we're all republicans with one goal - the unification of our country.

Locally, young Damien Mullan who had been co-opted in place of Aileen Mellon stood down from council with John McGowan co-opted in his place. What an asset John will be to our council. I look forward to seeing what he'll bring to the role.

With the 2022 Assembly Election just around the corner, the ballot boxes were scheduled for May 5, 2022 and both Ciara Ferguson and Padraig Delargy were running in the Foyle constituency. The party-initiated campaigns for its candidates, and canvassing began with a leaflet drop in every household in Ballyarnett and the new Skeoge estates. That year also saw over seven-thousand election leaflets delivered.

The next hurdle was ensuring everyone was registered to vote, as their vote was redundant otherwise. That year was particularly complicated as the Electoral Office had somehow wiped thousands off the electoral register and they'd need to reapply. If you ask me, governments seem to have deliberately made it harder to vote here in the North than in any other country. I wonder why?

In all my years fighting elections, I rarely saw the level of enthusiasm that I saw in 2022. Cumann members and our Comrades from Donegal stepped up to the mark as always, canvassing in the mornings, afternoons, and evenings. There were others who I felt could have been doing a lot more, but overall, it was a great campaign as people were determined to see Ciara and Padraig elected. Conscious of the last few years' disappointing election turn-out, people went that extra mile and worked overtime to make it count.

When the day of the 2022 Assembly Elections arrived, everybody gave 110 percent to make sure it was a success. When the polls closed that night, we felt satisfied that we'd given it all we could. Now all we could hope for was a good result in the ballot boxes.

The count came in, and Padraig topped the poll with 9,471 first preference votes, and Ciara came in third with 5,913 votes which was a fantastic result for the party in the city, and especially for the first-time runners. That election gave us the most seats in Stormont for the first time ever, and Michelle O'Neill returned as First Minister designate.

During the 2022/23 year of Derry City Council, Sandra Duffy became mayor of the city and what a fantastic mayor she was. I'd say Sandra was by far one of the best mayors we've had for a long time. She reached out to all the city and district and this popularity was clear in the 2023 May council election results. Sandra, John McGowan and Pat Murphy were selected to represent the party for the Ballyarnett DA and Sandra topped the poll with over 2,000 votes. John and Pat were elected too, winning back the seat we had lost previously.

History was made in those election results. No matter what happens in the future - a nationalist and more importantly, a republican – is now eligible to become First Minister for the first time. Calls and messages of congratulations came in from all over the country to Michelle and Marylou McDonald on this historical result. Of course, unionists still refuse to recognise a Sinn Féin first minister, but democracy is democracy. It also makes the call for a Border Poll stronger.

Since then, Sinn Féin has grown from strength to strength. and, after another huge gain in the local elections, Sinn Féin became the largest party in both local government and Stormont for the first time ever. Now the party has 144 councillors compared to the 105 seats returned in 2019.

It is now autumn 2023 and Stormont remains deadlocked over the NI Protocol. They can't accept the fall-out from a Brexit they voted for – a Brexit that has backfired for them and pushed us closer to a united Ireland than ever.

When the assembly does sit again, the DUP must accept a democratically elected nationalist First Minister, which will no doubt be another challenge. The party is again strong in Derry, and has overcome the problems that had previously stunted our potential

It's over twenty-five years since the Good Friday Agreement and numerous proposals for addressing legacy issues have come and gone, including policing reform, the Stormont House Agreement in 2014 and New Decade, New Approach in 2020.

One could be forgiven for thinking peace is assured, but I'm not sure that's the case. We are lacking in the broadest sense because unionists and the DUP can't move forward on some of the fundamental elements of the Good Friday Agreement, like justice, equality, and respect. After a hundred years of partition, of British occupation, and control of the north of Ireland - the only democratic solution is to end partition and acknowledge the right of all of the people of Ireland to exercise self-determination.

My vision of a new Ireland is one that welcomes and nurtures all traditions, cultures, and races and where all political views are respected. I think those conversations should begin now and we should be seriously planning for a time when the island can be united and what that means for each of us. The European Parliament said it no longer recognised the north of Ireland as part of the United Kingdom. I think it's time to try the only solution that hasn't been tried and unite our country.

As this account of my time ends, I see my life and the city differently. Sinn Féin have achieved what many thought impossible, and things are changing at last. The party in Derry has been through trying times, but beyond all that we must remember what we stand for.

We must remember ALL our friends and comrades who gave their lives for the struggle in one way or another. We must now move forward, as friends and comrades, to embrace the future and make things better for future generations.

It's incredible to stop and realise how far we have come, and that we're edging ever closer to our dream of a united Ireland in our time. It's not going to happen next week, but it will happen I am sure. We are in a generational change which cannot be stopped and for Sinn Féin as a party going forward united cannot be stopped.

An Deireadh (The End)